When the Ghost Screams

Also by Leslie Rule

Coast to Coast Ghosts: True Stories of Hauntings Across America

Ghosts Among Us: True Stories of Spirit Encounters

When the Ghost Screams

True Stories of Victims Who Haunt

Leslie Rule

**Andrews McMeel
Publishing, LLC**

Kansas City

ISBN-13: 978-0-7407-6175-1

Photography by Leslie Rule
Book design by Holly Camerlinck

For DaMeisha Bartunek

Contents

Foreword

by **Ann Rule**

Although my daughter Leslie is the ghost researcher in our family, the genres in which we write often overlap. She has helped people grieving over family members lost to murder, and I sometimes run into emissaries from that "other world," or talk to homicide detectives who use more than solid physical evidence to catch a killer.

As I write this, Leslie and I both had book deadlines that caught up with us on the same weekend. Mother and daughter, we are alike in our work habits in many ways. Although she writes at night and in the wee hours of the morning and I write during the daytime, we both tend to work slowly until we get close to the end of a book, and then we rev up our engines and sometimes it does seem as if an offscreen voice is dictating to us. But I don't think that's a ghost; at the most, it's our writing muse.

Even so, I often find connections or synchronicities. As it happens, the book I finished earlier today was about a sea captain who vanished inexplicably from his home on a foggy island in the San Juans off the coast of Washington State. Whether he was murdered or simply walked away from a life and a wife he could no longer bear is the mystery in my book. But there is little doubt that, ultimately, he did not survive. In the course of his sixty years at sea all over the world, he was a ship's pilot as well as a captain. These highly skilled men (and, today, women) guide mammoth ships safely into port through the narrowest of waterways. And he was the oldest pilot of them all: seventy-nine. Although his physical body was never found, his spirit survived. And on the very day that the person convicted of killing him died, another younger pilot stood exactly where the old pilot had once guided a ship. Indeed, it was the very same ship, with a different name.

"I felt his hand on my shoulder," the young pilot said, "as surely as if he really stood there. He's long dead wherever he is, but his spirit was on that ship."

But back to homicide detectives. In my early years as the Northwest reporter for *True Detective* and five other fact detective magazines, I realized I needed to go back to college and get a second major, this time in Crime Scene Investigation. I was also lucky enough to be invited to attend the King County, Washington, sheriff's two-week homicide investigation course that every rookie deputy had to attend.

One of the rules of thumb is that at least two detectives are required to work a murder scene; one picks up evidence and seals and labels it in plastic baggies, and the other makes notes. When they measure distances so that they can re-create the scene absolutely by triangulation to fixed points, there has to be an investigator on each end of the tape. Or one detective takes photographs or videotapes the scene, while the other keeps track of who arrives and who leaves.

I think most of us in the "rookie" class were surprised, then, when the detective sergeant who was our instructor told us, "I work homicide scenes alone. At least I start out that way. I want to listen to the victim . . ."

In the class, we darted our eyes at each other, wondering if he was kidding. But he was serious as he clicked the slide projector to bring up the image of a beautiful corpse, saying, "I talked to her for awhile, getting a fix on who was the last person she saw, trying to understand what had happened to her and why. However the other guys work murders, this is the way I begin. And it works for me."

As it turned out, the woman's husband had killed her in a jealous rage, and then arranged her body tenderly so that she would "look nice," as he said later.

I don't know if she really "talked" to the detective who taught our class, but he solved the case and he said that he had the sense of who her killer was from the very beginning.

There are many people who believe that inanimate objects can somehow retain dark and wicked acts that occurred around or because of them. Maybe I believe this too. I am not sure. When I attended the trial of Diane Downs in Eugene, Oregon, in 1984, for the book that became *Small Sacrifices*, one piece of physical evidence played a powerful if silent part in the prosecution's case. Diane, who was in love with a married man who didn't want children, stood accused of shooting her three children during a drive in the lonely countryside one May night. She apparently believed that if she didn't have a family, her lover would leave his wife and come to her.

Diane testified that a "bushy-haired stranger" had flagged her down, demanded her keys, and then shot her small children, killing one and critically injuring the other two. She had escaped with a gunshot wound to her lower arm.

Lane County detectives searched her town house and found a bronze unicorn statuette in a prominent place on her television set. A plate on the front was engraved with a date, the names, "Christie," "Cheryl," and "Danny," and the words "I love you, Mom." The date was five days earlier than the night of the shooting.

The investigators learned that Diane had taken her children to the Pacific Ocean and the Willamette River on the engraved date. She had driven around aimlessly, returning home close to midnight when her children were crying with exhaustion. The sheriff's men deduced that she had meant to kill them then but she had lost her nerve.

The prosecutor suggested that the unicorn was "fungible," a legal term that means one thing can be exchanged for another of like value. To Diane Downs, it seemed meant to take the place of three dead children. She would have their names and her memories, but not the burden or the responsibility of being a single mother, frustrated because she could not be with her lover.

Diane Downs's jury was convinced that that was the truth of the tragedy. The unicorn had meant death and murder.

Detective Doug Welch took custody of the unicorn after Diane was convicted and sent to prison. *Small Sacrifices* was published, and Welch thought that the bronze statuette would be an ideal birthday present for me, a souvenir of my first best-selling true crime book. He may not know until he reads this that I was horrified as I opened the heavy box he mailed to me. I was afraid of what I would find inside. And it was, indeed, the dreaded unicorn. I didn't want to seem ungrateful so I thanked him, ignoring my premonitions.

For me, the next three days were one mishap after another. First, I slipped on spilled water in the supermarket and hurt my back. While I was still limping, a drunk driver ran into the back of my car and did a lot of damage.

I had nightmares every night about murder, and I almost never have bad dreams about what I write. I've always believed that it's cathartic to write about the things that frighten me or make me sad. I get rid of the thoughts, and what might have become nightmares just flow out of the tips of my fingers into my computer and into a book. I don't have to let them take up space in my subconscious mind.

But with the unicorn sitting on my desk, I felt as though I had lost all protection from bad luck and evil itself. When my computer swallowed half a book and I barely got it back and my dog got sick, I made up my mind. I wrapped Diane Downs's unicorn up carefully and returned it to Doug Welch by Federal Express.

He has had it many years now, solved many more murders, and retired from his career as a police officer without incident. And I'm grateful for that because he's a very nice man. If Diane had the power to put a hex on anyone, I'm sure she would have picked Doug because he was the one who brought in the most compelling evidence against her.

Maybe it was me and my spooky feeling about having the unicorn in my house; maybe I drew the bad luck to myself. But there are simply objects that I don't want around me. I "accidentally" erased the tape recording where Ted Bundy confesses to murder. I didn't do it deliberately, but I pushed the "record" button instead of "forward," and taped over his voice. Why did I do that when it would have been a compelling addition to my lectures? And why have I never tried to get another copy of that tape? I think I know.

After Ted was executed and I was adding an update chapter to the *Stranger Beside Me*, I found that I could not work with his picture on the shelf behind me. I put it away. Although I still have a few dozen letters he wrote to me from prison, I don't keep them where I live.

My own most memorable experience with another time and another place—or maybe I should say it's the same place—happened about a dozen years ago.   I can't really explain it, although I have tried. I was driving on the Alaskan Way Viaduct, a double-decker road that divides downtown Seattle and the waterfront district. As always, I shifted my gaze momentarily from the road ahead to Eliott Bay and then to the skyscrapers that now proliferate in the downtown area. The Smith Tower, once the tallest building west of the Mississippi River, has been eclipsed by shining blue and black aquamarine glass-fronted buildings, its peaked top diminished and humbled as the old building seems shrunken among newer architectural upstarts.

 As I looked at the downtown skyline on the day I recall, it suddenly became flat and one dimensional. It was no longer dominated by many different colors but had become sepia toned like a very old newspaper, faded by long time passing. In fact, it seemed to me that I had flashed back to the way the earlier city had looked.

Aloud, I said, "Oh, Leander, who would ever have thought it!"

And then I said, aloud again, to myself, "Well, Ann, where on earth did that come from?"

For a matter of seconds, I found myself a century back in time. I was a woman named Beulah Carmody and a man whose first name was Leander was my husband. (I had never heard of the name before.) We owned a small, dark store that sold groceries and other items. It was right on the mudflats, and it smelled of smoke from a combination cookstove/heating stove. An oilskin drape separated our living quarters from the store. I was aware that I was not a pretty woman but short and round with dark hair pulled into a bun. And I had a baby in a cradle close by the stove.

Leander, on the other hand, was a handsome man with light brown hair and a luxuriant mustache, thin and too tall. He wore a light-colored shirt with his sleeves rolled up and suspenders. I sensed that we were happily married. I absorbed all of that information in an extremely short time.

And then I blinked. The sepia-toned flat view of Seattle vanished, and I was back in the twentieth century. My car hadn't moved more than fifty feet and it was time to ease right onto the Seneca Street off-ramp.

It never happened before and it's never happened again. I wasn't thinking about history when I seemed to have slipped through a curtain in time, and I don't understand why I did. Maybe I saw ghosts of someone from the early days. Maybe I did have another life as a homely woman named Beulah Carmody a few lives ago.

Leslie thinks I may have been tuning into the ghosts of old Seattle. A few years after my experience, she made an interesting discovery as she researched the ghosts who roam Pioneer Square. A man named Leander Terry was part of the Denny party who founded Seattle in 1851. The Terry family did have a store on the mudflats, but so far we have found no mention of Beulah Carmody.

Was I married to Leander in another life? All I know is that when I arrived in Seattle after having been born in Michigan, and growing up in Pennsylvania and Oregon, I felt as if I had come home. I knew I belonged here, and even though I have to travel a lot in my career, I'm always so glad to come back to where I belong.

I will continue to research the criminal mind and forensic science and strive to tell the victims' stories, but I will always encourage my daughter in her studies of the things we cannot quite prove, or see, or document with complete accuracy.

Introduction

When the ghost screams, we seldom hear, for the sound is drummed out by the beating of our hearts. We are alive, you and I. Our world is filled with machines and schedules and people with pulses who speak loudly, even when they don't have much to say.

Yet the ghost calls out. Sometimes if we stop to listen, we hear its voice choked by the rustle of the leaves or harmonizing with the train whistle in the distance.

Or sometimes it wakes us at night.

It wakes us because it was once as we are—snuggled in our beds with the night shut safely outside. It had a body, too, and perhaps nice shiny shoes lined up in the closet or maybe just one tattered pair of sneakers tossed carelessly in the corner. It had an alarm clock and someplace to be. Eventually. For every living person has somewhere to go. School. Work. Or downstairs for a piece of toast with marmalade and butter.

The ghost once did these things too. It likely had the same mundane attitude about life that most people do. Until life is taken away.

Suddenly the once-living being exists in a place that we can only imagine. Depending on one's religious view, the dead one might be suspended in time or shuttled off to a wondrous place. The theories, of course, are widely varied.

I do not know or pretend to know what happens when we die. Still, I hear the ghost scream. I hear the screaming and am compelled to write the stories of those whose lives were snatched away. They are the murder victims, the ones who roam restlessly. They are the headliners of this book.

A leading theory among my peers says that the souls of those who die violently are prone to remain earthbound. And indeed, my research indicates that the sites with the most paranormal activity are most often tied to deadly violence, especially unsolved homicides.

If each page of this book is a stage, then the ghosts made from murder are the stars. Their haunts are often populated with those who died much gentler deaths, and they, too, will make appearances as the stories unfold.

Frequently we find that haunted places are crowded with a number of ghosts from a variety of eras. Some speculate that an earthbound spirit "opens the door" for others to move through and join him. If this is the case, then I wonder if it is the ghost who is most rooted to this plane who opens the door for the others. In any event, the murdered ghosts' "friends" will be included here.

They are clamoring for attention now. In hotels and cafés and hospitals and schools and within private residences, they are trying to make us notice. So listen carefully as you read their stories and perhaps you, too, will hear the ghost scream.

When the Ghost Screams

one

The Ice Files

When it comes to haunting, there seems to be no statute of limitations. A crime may have occurred a hundred years ago in a particular place, but the environment seems to cling to the bad energy as if it were yesterday.

Maybe a detective believed he was "hot on the heels" of a criminal a century ago, only to become discouraged as the trail went cold. With the case unsolved for decades, the detective and even the criminal eventually die, leaving only a cold file stashed in a forgotten filing cabinet.

And, finally, all who remembered the crime are gone, and the case has turned to ice. These ice files might freeze right into obscurity if not for the phenomena connected with them.

Hauntings prompt ghost detectives to crack through the veneer of the past, to dig up archives to help us understand. Again and again, we find that extremely haunted places tend to be the sites of past violence. And the most active sites are often the scenes of unsolved homicides. It is as if the dead victims are waiting for justice.

It does not seem to matter how much time has passed. The murdered don't seem to know or care that they've been relegated to the ice files.

Here are a few stories of spirits who move in the cold realm of cases unsolved.

Lady in Green

It is March 1956 in Avard, Oklahoma. The high school gymnasium resonates with the sights, sounds, and scents typical of school gyms across America. Gangly teenage boys with crew cuts zip across the basketball court, their shouts punctuating the rhythmic bounce of the ball. The sharp scent of rubber and sweat permeate the air.

Flash ahead half a century to 2006 and the scene changes. The gymnasium is all that is left of the school, long ago razed when the tiny town no longer had the youth to warrant it. The old walls now hold Vina Rae's Grill 'n' Graze, an unpretentious café where owners Nan Wheatley and Debra Campbell serve up chicken-fried steak, mashed potatoes and gravy, and wedges of hot apple pie.

The long-legged boys have been usurped by hungry families; the thump of the basketball by friendly conversation and the soft clink of silverware; and the smell of rubber and sweat by brewing coffee, grilling hamburger, and burning hair.

Burning hair?

Yes, sometimes the terrible inexplicable odor overwhelms visitors. "The first time I smelled it, it made me sick," confided Nan Wheatley, explaining that when the scent materializes, it is always confined to a very small area. "If you step away from the spot, you can't smell it."

It is just one of the many calling cards of the ghost. She was born Mildred Ann Newlin on Christmas Day in 1933. She grew up and got married in 1955. Nine months later, on a crisp March afternoon, small-town innocence was lost forever to Avard, Oklahoma.

Mildred was sweet and lovely with a shy smile and very petite at just five feet two inches and one hundred pounds. She was a twenty-two-year-old senior at Northwestern Oklahoma State University at Alva and happily married to twenty-six-year-old Avard High School teacher and basketball coach Richard D. Reynolds. "They were exceptional people," said Nan, adding that everyone called Richard "Dee" and that Mildred went by "Ann." "Dee was very close to some of my family members."

Their future should have been bright. Ann looked forward to graduating and becoming a schoolteacher, and she and Dee dreamed of having four children. They would raise them in the land they loved. But fate had a heartless plan for them.

It was Tuesday, March 13, just after noon when Ann finished her morning classes at Alva, climbed into her 1949 Chevrolet Tudor, and began her half-hour journey toward Avard High School to meet her husband.

She never made it.

We will never know what thoughts were in her head as she drove the long dirt road toward Avard. The last thing she saw was the familiar northwestern Oklahoma prairie with its miles of flat wheat fields, and then her killer or killers.

It was a little after one p.m. when farmer Loren Goucher was riding his tractor and noticed clouds of black smoke billowing in the distance. When he investigated, he was shocked to find a car on fire on the Alva-Avard Road. The blazing automobile straddled a shallow ditch, its rear wheels embedded in the sand. The front door hung open.

Loren smelled burning flesh as he moved through the intense heat. He crept close enough to see a charred body on the front seat. He rushed to the Alva police station.

Coach Dee Reynolds soon learned the horrific news. While he was at school, his poor bride had suffered a terrible death. At first investigators thought it had been an accident. Somehow Ann had lost control of her car and hit a blackjack tree. When she tried to drive away, the car had burst into flames. Cans of brake fluid and gasoline in the trunk had accelerated the fire.

Family members confirmed that Ann did indeed have dizzy spells and could have been overtaken by one while driving. Yet there were so many odd elements to the puzzle.

Her right shoe, splattered with blood, had been found 256 feet in front of the car beside a patch of tall grass that had been mashed flat as if someone had lain there, possibly during an attack. Ann's charred coat was discovered ten feet behind the car. A button, perhaps ripped from her blouse or an assailant's shirt, was also found outside the car.

The Chevy had burned bumper to bumper, as if it had been doused with an accelerant. The tires had burned, and the engine compartment was scorched. The temperature had reached 1,700 degrees, hot enough to shatter the auto's windows. It did not make sense that a spontaneous fire starting in the trunk could do so much damage. All of these facts were brought before a jury to determine whether the case warranted further investigation.

Dr. Max Shideler, who had performed the autopsy, told the jury that Ann had suffered skull fractures that could have resulted from blows to the head—or from the intense heat in the blazing car.

There had been possible sightings of another vehicle near the scene, and a second set of tire tracks suggested she may have been run off the road. Then there was the question of bullet casings found nearby.

In the end, the jury decided that a homicide had taken place.

It was difficult for Ann's family to imagine that anyone had deliberately hurt her. Mr. Reynolds said that his pretty wife had no enemies.

It looked as if Ann was killed for the same sad reason that so many others are. She was a vulnerable female in the wrong place at the wrong time when a monster who could not control his rage happened upon her. Someone had battered Ann and then tried to incinerate all clues. All of the newlyweds' dreams had gone up in smoke.

Detectives spent five days on campus interviewing dozens of Ann's classmates, but no one admitted to knowing a thing about her death. Despite a long investigation, her murder has yet to be solved.

Today Nan Wheatley shakes her head as she ponders the icy cold case. "I wish that they had had the forensic technology that they do today," she said.

❧

When Nan and Debra opened Vina Rae's Grill 'n' Graze a decade ago, the last thing they expected was to share the place with ghosts. In fact, ghosts were something they gave little thought to—until an unexpected visitor appeared.

Shortly after Vina Rae's opened for business, Debra was surprised to see a customer seated at a table. Why didn't I hear her come in, she wondered as she glanced at the pretty young woman in green. Normally the cowbell clanged loudly whenever someone stepped through the door.

The woman was intent on adjusting her skirt and made no eye contact with Debra. "I turned away to get my order pad and then turned back to take her order," Debra explained. But when she turned back, she was in for a shock. Debra stared, her pen poised and her mouth agape, at the empty table. The lady in green had vanished as quickly as she had appeared.

A chill crept down her neck. "I asked Nan what Ann Reynolds looked like," she said. The description matched, right down to the short auburn hair. And when Nan and Debra learned that Ann had been wearing green the day she was murdered, they were sure that it was she who had visited.

Fifty years ago Ann had been headed to the man she loved when evil intervened. Was she still trying to find him? Her destination on March 13, 1956, had been the high school. Had her spirit continued on, even as her body lay burning? Had she entered the school on her death day only to find that Dee could not feel her arms around him? That she was unable to wipe the tears of grief from his eyes?

The spirit of Mildred Ann Reynolds may be stuck in the old gymnasium, the place where she surely once sat in the bleachers and cheered on her husband's team. Does she understand that it is no longer a basketball court? Is she aware that her widowed husband eventually remarried and years later died of a heart attack?

Perhaps Ann does know that time has passed, and that things have changed. Perhaps she simply wants her case solved. Perhaps she is seeking justice.

Locals claim that most folks in town know who the killer is. In fact, rumor has it that two men were involved. With dangerous killers at large, it is understandable that they are reluctant to speak of it. Does that fact frustrate Ann's spirit?

Was it Ann who threw the sponge at Nan? "I was alone in the kitchen," said Nan, recalling the day that a sponge sailed through the air at her. She has gotten used to the sudden knocks on the wall, the inexplicable jingle of silverware, and the shadowy figures who move through her peripheral vision. "But there was a time," admitted Nan, "when I did not like to be alone in the building."

She and her mother, Ramona Wheatley, were both shaken up when a spooky apparition made an appearance. Nan's mom, now deceased, was a levelheaded woman, so when she told her daughter what she had seen, Nan believed her.

"She hollered at me and said a headless woman came through a wall and floated into the kitchen," remembered Nan.

Even more frightening was the night that Nan was locking the back door when unseen hands grabbed her roughly by the shoulders and threw her down the hall. She picked herself up off the floor, unhurt but stunned. "I didn't tell anyone about it for a long time," admitted Nan, who feared people would think she was losing her mind.

Sometimes the sound of footsteps would echo in the empty hallway, and the freezer would be mysteriously rearranged.

Later, while seeking answers to the strange goings on, Nan invited paranormal researchers and psychics to investigate. When a psychic described an angry man named Isaac who stalked the premises, Nan was stunned. The description matched the entity that she had picked up on—a gloomy aggressive old man.

"The psychic did a cleansing of the building," said Nan. "Ann's ghost stayed, but Isaac moved out to the vacant house across the street."

A woman named Mary was visiting Avard for the first time and was a passenger in a car when she glanced at the dilapidated house and noticed a man sitting in a La-Z-Boy chair on the porch. "He didn't look like he'd be too tall, maybe average height," she said, adding that he was either bald or gray and that his face was contorted into an angry expression. "It was not evil, but hateful," she said. "He looked like he was in his late fifties or early sixties. He wore dark pants and a light button-up shirt."

This researcher has discovered two Isaacs did live and die in Arvard long ago. I've yet to learn details about their lives.

Back in the Isaacs' time, Avard had a heftier population, but over the years it has dwindled, and today Avard is a ghost town. "We have only about twenty people living here," said Nan.

Twenty live people—the dead ones are too many to count. "We've had psychics tell us we have wall-to-wall ghosts in the café," said Nan. "They say that the café is a portal to the other side where ghosts pass through."

Though it is an interesting idea, it cannot, of course, be confirmed. While psychics can sometimes be dead-on, they rarely have all of the answers. One that Nan consulted also tuned in to Ann Reynolds, and asked her why she had not moved on. "Ann told her she was still here because she wanted to know 'why they have done this to me,'" said Nan.

They.

The use of a plural supports the rumor that two attackers are guilty.

The killers are old men by now. Do they still roam freely through the area? Do they feel even a twinge of remorse when they drive past the spot on the lonely road where they savagely attacked an innocent person?

Mildred Ann Reynolds was charred beyond recognition, her right leg burned off to the knee. The woman who loved children never got to teach and nurture the countless students who would surely have loved her back. Is it too much for her to ask for some kind of justice?

Chances are she will continue to appear at Vina Rae's Grill 'n' Graze, toss sponges, jiggle the silverware, and rap on the walls until the case is solved.

We are rooting for you, Ann.

Only a Moment

A gentle snow fell upon Miami University in Oxford, Ohio. It looked as if Ronald Tammen had stepped out of his dorm for only a moment. Despite the cold night, the 19-year-old business major had not taken his coat. He'd also left his wallet and car keys behind and the radio playing. His psychology book lay open on the desk, as if he'd been interrupted in the middle of studying. If students passing by Fisher Hall had glanced up at the window, they would have seen that the lights were burning in room 225 of the old ivy-covered building.

Ron's roommate was not alarmed when he returned to find him gone. Other than Ron's absence, nothing in the room was unusual. Surely he would be back in a moment. But that moment has stretched into decades. For when Ron Tammen left that room, it was April 19, 1953. He vanished like a snowflake in a flame, never to be seen again.

A handsome, muscular young man, Ron was a varsity wrestler and the residence hall adviser. The evening of his disappearance he'd played the string bass with his dance band, the Campus Owls, and had returned to his dorm about 8:30 p.m. His 1938 Chevrolet sat outside for the rest of the evening.

Who can begin to imagine the heartbreak for Ron's family? His younger brother was also a student at Miami and must have been beside himself. His parents were frantic as they agonized over his fate, wondering if there was any truth to the speculation that he was an amnesia victim. And they surely felt a spark of hope when a woman from a nearby town came forward to say that a man who matched Ron's description had knocked on her door in the early morning of April 20. The young man, she said, had a streak of dirt across his face and appeared dazed as he asked her for directions to the bus stop.

A tragedy for his friends and family, the disappearance became a celebrated legend for future students at Miami University who dubbed him "the Phantom of Oxford."

While many argue that Ron probably lost his memory and is still alive today, others think he died and remains on campus as a spirit.

Fisher Hall was a creepy old place that already had a reputation for being haunted when Ron resided there. The enormous structure had been dedicated on September 3, 1856, as the Oxford Female College. Heralded as the finest college building in the West, the features included a dining room and a chapel, which seated eight hundred. There was room for two hundred students to live, and they were excited to have the luxury of hot and cold running water.

The building had many incarnations, including time as the Oxford Hotel and later as a mental asylum. When the university purchased the building in 1925, it came with a few forgotten artifacts that students stumbled upon over the years. They shuddered when they found the old straitjackets and imagined the troubled souls once confined within the brick walls.

Ron's vanishing added to the mysterious ambience. When the leaves turned golden and began to drift from the elm trees, students were both thrilled and frightened to learn that a ghost had been seen in the formal gardens behind Fisher Hall.

When they heard the apparition singing, witnesses felt cold to the bone. Perhaps it was only another student playing a joke, but when skeptics gave chase, it eluded them, melting into the night as easily as it had appeared.

Some insisted that the figure had to be Ron's ghost. He was, after all, a musician who expressed himself through song. Others smirked and said it was a prank.

Pranks were not unusual among the students. In fact, on the very evening that Ron vanished, he'd found his bed filled with dead fish. He was last seen when he fetched clean sheets before returning to his room. As he gathered the clean bedding, he'd mentioned that he was tired and was going to bed early.

What could have changed his plans?

Was there another practical joke the night Ron disappeared—a prank that went horribly wrong, with the popular sophomore ending up injured or worse? If a joke did indeed get out of hand, the perpetrators weren't talking.

A few years after Ron went missing, the upper floors of Fisher Hall were deserted after they became so rundown that they were deemed unsafe, and the first floor became home to the university's theater. The theater students insisted there was a ghost in their midst. Some were simply annoyed when items inexplicably vanished—a common occurrence in haunted places. Others were afraid to be in the building alone. Shadows darted past the windows, they said, and they were troubled by the sounds of muffled voices. No one could quite make out what was being said. Was it the Phantom of Oxford trying to tell them something?

Fisher Hall eventually fell into complete disrepair, and the once-grand building was used for storage. Those who walked by often felt eyes upon them and quickened their pace as they glanced up nervously at the black windows. Braver students sometimes broke into the haunted building, half hoping to encounter a specter. The story of the missing boy's ghost became a favorite Halloween topic for the local media.

Ronald's parents died without learning the fate of their beloved son.

Fisher Hall was demolished in 1979, the fine, pink dust from the bricks floating away on the breeze with old secrets. Today, the Marcum Conference Center occupies the spot.

Ronald Henry Tammen Jr. is still missing.

For more information on Ronald Tammen and other missing people, visit the Doe Network at www.doenetwork.org.

Ghosts of Miami University

With its forested landscape and silver streams, Miami University in Oxford, Ohio, is known as one of the loveliest college campuses in America. Lovely and spooky. Many of the grand old buildings are shrouded in mysteries and crawling with ghosts. Some say that the restless spirits originate from a century-old tragedy in Brice Hall. The girls were in tears, and the boys shook their heads in disbelief when a favorite teacher, Professor Henry Snyder, was found dead in his Brice Hall chemistry laboratory.

Students and teachers whispered about the "suicide." What had driven Professor Snyder to ingest a fatal dose of potassium cyanide? The September 14, 1898, death raised suspicions, however. Some wondered if his flamboyant wife, Minnie, had murdered him.

The couple was a study in contrasts. He was the typical professor, while Minnie was a sexy siren who loved to dress like a gypsy and sing on stage. That, of course, is not enough to suggest someone is a killer, but the stain of suspicion darkened when she married her husband's lab assistant, William Pugh.

Had the seductive Mrs. Snyder lured William into the murder plot? Had he administered the poison? Twenty years later, William mysteriously vanished and was reportedly never seen again.

Did William's ghost, realizing that he too was the victim of a black widow, return to the campus to commiserate with poor Professor Snyder's ghost?

While she was not a killer or a victim, Helen Peabody's ghost frightens some students the most. An outspoken critic of coeducation and the principal of the neighboring school, the Western Female Seminary, Helen was strict and formidable.

The boys who slipped onto her campus to meet girls knew they had to sneak past the stern woman who sent many of them racing back to their dorms. In Helen's time, proper young ladies did not spend unescorted time with men. And she certainly did not want her female students attending classes with males. She surely would have been appalled when the two schools merged.

Seminary Hall, built in 1855, was once part of Helen Peabody's campus and was renamed for her in 1905. Students insist that her ghost haunts Peabody Hall. An inexplicable low guttural sound is sometimes heard, and the shower is known to turn itself on.

Two boys living in the hall were literally shaken up when their entire room experienced an earthquake not felt anywhere else. They stared, wide-eyed, as their furniture shook and items spilled from their desktops.

Students often hurry past the big portrait of Helen in the building's foyer. Her eyes, they say, follow them. And legend has it that when someone has done something of which Helen would have disapproved, the portrait's eyes blink as the guilty party goes by.

Some say that Reid Hall is also haunted. Students report phantom footsteps in empty rooms and a pair of bloody handprints on a door.

Students say the ghost of Helen Peabody, once principal of Western Female Seminary, seems to be watching them. This antique postcard shows the magnificent building where the stern opponent of co-education lives on as a ghost. (author's collection)

The prints, they insist, will not wash away and were made decades ago by a student shot and killed when he tried to break up a fight.

A May 9, 1959, article in the *Vidette Messenger* verified the murder when it reported the death of twenty-year-old Roger T. Sayles from Gary, Indiana. Roger was entertaining his mother, who was visiting for Mother's Day, when he heard a commotion in the hallway.

He left his room to find two men arguing over a girl they were both dating. Eighteen-year-old Henry Lucas from Springfield, Ohio, opened fire, wounding his rival and killing Roger with two bullets.

Police searched the campus, but the killer was not found until seven hours after the shooting when a student in Ogden Hall went to make a call and found Henry slumped over in a phone booth. He'd shot himself in the head. He was rushed to the hospital in critical condition and later died.

Is it Henry or Roger who stalks Reid Hall?

Perhaps it is both of them, still trying to figure out what went wrong on that tragic Mother's Day.

A **Dark** Premonition

The students in the Technological Institute huddled over their books, trying to ignore the odd noises that emanated from the walls. They did not have time to entertain the idea of ghosts or to discuss silly legends. They were, after all, serious pupils of one of the most selective colleges in the country, Northwestern University in Evanston, Illinois, just north of Chicago.

Sarah Bailey, however, managed to pry a student or two away from their books long enough to get the scoop for the school newspaper, the *Daily Northwestern*, in October 2004. Late-night studiers, she wrote, sometimes heard the sound of flasks and glasses clinking against each other. The noise was followed by a rattle and then an indefinable whisper.

The haunted Northwestern University is crawling with ghosts. (1921 yearbook)

More than one student reporter has speculated about the identities of the ghosts who inhabit the old college on the shore of Lake Michigan, entertaining various legends, such as the one that says the Tech Building ghost is a 1950s chemistry student who drank a tube of cyanide after his doctoral dissertation was rejected. Others believe that two female students committed suicide in the late 1800s after their fiancées deserted them. Witnesses swear they've heard the disembodied voices of the spirits weeping and commiserating with each other.

Another specter is said to be that of a heartbroken student who hung himself in the University Hall's bell tower. And some say that Annie May Swift, an 1880s student who succumbed to an illness, still roams the campus and has a special attachment to the building named after her.

This writer, however, made one of her frequent forages into forgotten archives to finger an entirely different restless spirit. The sad story was buried so deeply that few on campus are aware of it. I found it by accident. I was researching another haunted location when a shocking news story surfaced. It chronicled the sort of death that often results in earthbound spirits. My investigation into the ghosts of

The Annie May Swift Hall at Northwestern University, depicted in this antique image, is home to the ghost of young Annie who succumbed to illness while attending college here. (author's collection)

Northwestern University was backward. First I found the death, and then I looked for ghosts where the tragedy had occurred.

My sixth sense told me that while many spirits may inhabit the campus, a 1921 student was surely among them. Those familiar with

Northwestern University as it appeared when one student mysteriously vanished. (1922 yearbook)

my books know that I am only slightly shy about admitting that my intuition sometimes guides me as I track ghosts. And in this instance, that sixth sense felt as sharp as the one the victim himself felt when he made a gloomy prediction.

Freshman Leighton Mount had a special affection for an older woman, twenty-four-year-old Doris Fuchs, who did not return his feelings. "You made me love you," he wrote in a last note to her in September 1921.

"We were what you might call pals," Doris said in 1923.

Was Leighton simply trying to get her attention when he spoke to her about ways he could end his life? He dismissed the idea of drowning, because his body would resurface, she remembered. She was so used to his ramblings that at first she did not take him that seriously when he told her that he would "disappear during rush." Doris heard the statement as a half-hearted suicide threat. Was it a threat, or was it a premonition?

Leighton must have had reservations about the wild week of hazing, because his mother advised him that he had better participate, or he would "look like a sissy."

The barbaric "fight week" pitted freshmen and sophomore males against each other in tortuous "pranks." Did Leighton and his roommate, Roscoe Fitch, really have a choice? The rowdy, testosterone-driven event rushed over the campus like a tidal wave, picking up everything in its path and leaving the hapless wounded in its wake.

Some of the students were terrorized in the lake. Student Arthur Persinger, for instance, "was tied to a plank which was placed parallel with the water, and so low over it that the waves would splash over his face," according to one witness.

Young men kidnapped and tied each other up, sometimes abandoning angry and embarrassed students naked and far from campus. Almost everyone seemed to get through the September 1921 rush OK—everyone except for Leighton Mount.

Just as he had told Doris he would, Leighton disappeared.

At first, none of the other students would admit to having any idea of what had happened to him. But then Northwestern student and star athlete Charles Palmer, who worked at a bakery, told a coworker that he knew where Leighton was. When she pressed Palmer for details, he clammed up.

As Leighton's parents hired a private investigator, rumors circulated. Students told the university authorities that Leighton had been kidnapped by a newspaper reporter who was keeping him hidden. The reporter, they said, would eventually release him and get a great scoop for his newspaper.

Fifteen months went by with no word from Leighton, and then, at Christmastime, his parents received a telegram, signed "Leighton."

Was he alive? Or was someone trying to throw them off the trail?

In April 1923 another fight week turned tragic when Louis Aubere was killed in a car wreck. The cars were loaded with students involved in the rush, and some witnesses said that the crash was deliberate.

As students were grieving, a grisly discovery was made. A twelve-year-old boy went down to the lakeshore to play by the Lake Street Pier, south of the college campus. Puzzled by the odd bones he found beneath the pier, he took one home to show his mother. She called the police.

Leighton Mount had been found.

The bone the kid retrieved was one of Leighton's shin bones. Leighton's mother identified bits of clothing and a belt buckle, stamped with the initials L.M. Leighton's dentist made a positive identification.

While students said the death was a suicide, there was no discounting the rotted bits of rope found with the skeleton. It was the same type of rope that the boys used when they bound each other during rush.

Prosecutor Robert Crowe argued that Leighton had been kidnapped at midnight on Wednesday, September 21, 1921. The hazers had tied him beneath the pier and, when they returned the next day, found him dead. They had then made a pact to keep the death a secret. Now, twenty months later, dozens of people were subpoenaed as authorities demanded the truth in court.

The truth, however, was difficult to pinpoint. Some of the students changed their stories—including Leighton's roommate, Roscoe Fitch. Newspapers reported that after four trying hours and eight versions of his account, Roscoe burst into tears and cried, "I'll lose my credits! I'll

All-American boy Chuck Palmer may have had guilty knowledge of a cruel death. (1922 yearbook)

be kicked out of school if I tell! I dare not talk for I have been warned by men at the top to keep quiet, and I must do so!"

The school president himself, Walter Dill Scott, had his character called into question when it was implied that he had known more about Leighton's disappearance than he'd admitted. His detractors questioned why fifteen students had allegedly been mysteriously expelled immediately after the young man vanished.

In the end, a grand jury concluded that Leighton had indeed died by the hands of others.

News of a promising lead appeared in the July 17, 1923, issue of the *Indianapolis Daily Star* when a witness claimed that he had watched a group of men lower Leighton beneath the pier. The case, the paper said, may soon reopen. An archive search produced no more accounts of the case, and Leighton Mount's name dropped from the news.

The ivy on the old buildings grew thicker, the trees towered higher, alumni lived out their lives, and Leighton Mount was forgotten. The guilty walked free.

Some of the guilty must have felt remorse as they lived out their lives, the secret a prickly bur in their sides as they tried to forget. If still alive, the culprits would be near one hundred years old. Perhaps one with guilty knowledge told someone. And maybe that someone was a son or daughter who will now come forward with the information—especially when they learn that Leighton may still be in pain.

Most of those who loved Leighton are dead. Does he know that? Or is he stuck in the nightmare of a September morning in 1921? Is he still trying to escape his terrifying, watery grave where he was so callously abandoned until his last breath was replaced by cold lake water, and the skin floated from his bones?

Imagine, the terrorized spirit, trying to make his way back to campus. Imagine it, and you will very likely come up with an image that is much like the apparition seen near campus.

They call him "Seaweed Charlie."

Chicago ghost researcher Richard Crowe is well aware of the specter seen near the Evanston campus. Despite his grasp of Chicago history and the fact that he is related to the prosecutor who handled the fatal hazing case, the murder of Leighton Mount was buried so deeply that even Crowe hadn't heard of it. Yet he had known about "Seaweed Charlie" for years.

The tortured spirit is seen both crawling and walking from the water by Sheridan Road, near the Lake Street Pier where Leighton met his fate. Witnessed by many over the decades, the description does not vary, said Richard Crowe. One encounter occurred on a summer night in 1993, he told me. "Two girls, Lisa Becker and Jenny Trisko, were driving south along Sheridan Road around midnight," he said. "Suddenly they noticed the car in front of them swerving, as if to avoid something in the road."

Students enjoy playing in the lake, ignoring the dark secrets beneath the surface. (1922 yearbook)

There in the middle of the street was a man wearing a heavy trench coat. He had come from the direction of the lake.

"It was too nice [outside] to be wearing a coat," Lisa told Richard. Jenny said that the man was tall and thin and glowing. The ethereal being emanated an eerie light as he lumbered across the road. The girls had never heard of the Sheridan Road ghost, and when they excitedly described their encounter to friends, they learned that the mother of Jenny's boyfriend had seen the specter at the same spot ten years earlier.

When Richard Crowe speculated on the identity of the ghost, he had several ideas, including the theory that the ghost belonged to an instructor from the Glenview Naval Air Station who crashed his plane in the lake in May 1951.

My research confirmed the plane crash, along with details about two rescuers who drowned while trying to retrieve the pilot's body. They were on the lake just off campus when their boat capsized.

According to Richard, some who have seen the Sheridan Road ghost say that he is dripping with seaweed.

The Evanston, Illinois, campus, shown here in a vintage postcard, is lovely but filled with ghosts who carry dark secrets. (author's collection)

Are any of these men "Seaweed Charlie?"

Maybe. But what about the fact that the ghost is encountered around midnight, the same time that Leighton suffered his fate? Weigh the terror that was surely suffered by each lake victim, and Leighton wins the dismal contest.

Bound for hours beneath the pier in icy darkness, he was alone with his own tormented thoughts. What did he think of in his last moments? Did he think of Doris and how he would never again see her lovely smile? Did he imagine the grief his parents would feel if he let the lake take him?

Discovered dead and blue, he was further insulted by the cover-up. If there was ever a candidate for a spirit to remain earthbound, Leighton is it.

If you should travel along Sheridan Road, say a prayer for Leighton Mount as you pass the Lake Street Pier. If you should see the wet and glowing ghost, do not be afraid. It is probably just Leighton, a naïve young man in love with a girl named Doris.

Restless Victims

Are the ghosts of murdered people really more prone to stay earthbound?

Yes, according to Richard Crowe, Chicago's original ghost hunter. Leading ghost tours for three decades, the author of *Chicago's Street Guide to the Supernatural* frequently makes the connection between murder and ghosts.

He points to the case of Bobby Franks, the thirteen-year-old victim in a 1924 "thrill kill."

The murder made headlines not just because of the viciousness of the killing, but because both the victim and the killers were the sons of Chicago millionaires.

Nathan Leopold, eighteen, and his partner in crime, Richard Loeb, seventeen, had been planning to kill someone for months before accosting Bobby as he walked home from Harvard School on the southwest side of Chicago, explained Richard Crowe.

Bobby was Richard Loeb's second cousin, so the boy probably was not alarmed to see the familiar face peering from the car as it pulled up beside him. Relative or not, the sociopaths did not care. They thirsted for blood and took the opportunity to make their twisted fantasy a reality.

They brutally killed Bobby and dumped him in a culvert, where he was found so quickly that the ransom note was just being delivered to his parents' home.

A tip from a chauffeur led police to the rich boys. When a pair of tortoise-shell eyeglasses were found near the culvert, their prescription was matched to the pair worn by Leopold. Though he claimed that he'd lost them while in the area bird-watching, evidence against the teens mounted. Each blamed the other for the murder. In the end they were both convicted but escaped execution due to the expert defense by famous attorney Clarence Darrow.

While Darrow was fighting for the lives of the teenage killers, State's Attorney Robert E. Crowe was in Bobby's corner.

Robert and Richard Crowe are branches from the same family tree. Their roots are in Tipperary, Ireland, and it seems they have a karmic connection, each ending up in Chicago as a voice for murder victims. While Robert worked to put killers behind bars, Richard tells the stories of the restless spirits of the slain.

Was the spirit of Bobby Franks aware of this link when Richard Crowe visited his crypt in Rosehill Cemetery? Did he recognize the younger Crowe as the relative of the man who fought so vehemently to avenge his death?

It was 1988 when Richard Crowe, along with a cemetery caretaker, visited Bobby's grave. Richard told me he walked up to the door of the crypt and tried the handle, even though he did not expect it to be unlocked.

The caretaker gasped as the normally locked door creaked open. "Maybe the ghost of Bobby wants you to go in!" he exclaimed.

Richard entered and said a prayer for the soul of Bobby.

Afterward, as he stared solemnly at the cold, gray crypt, the caretaker shared some fascinating history. Years earlier, cemetery workers had frequently seen a boy wandering near the crypt. As they approached, the youngster would vanish. Everyone said it was the ghost of Bobby Franks. Interestingly, the ghost did not settle down until his killers met their own deaths.

Despite the fact they were incarcerated, the two enjoyed special privileges. "They had the run of the prison," said Richard. "They had special meals and private dining in the officers' lounge."

Richard Loeb died from razor cuts after a fight in the shower in 1936. Nathan Leopold, paroled in 1958, succumbed to heart failure in 1971. It was only then that the ghost sightings of Bobby Franks stopped.

Another Chicago area ghost, however, is not at rest.

"The murder of Emily Keseg is one of the area's most baffling mysteries," said Richard Crowe. An eighteen-year-old freshman in the fall of 1969, Emily attended classes at Morton College in Cicero, Illinois. At that time, Richard explained, the new college had not been built, so sessions were held at Morton East High School.

Emily was a quiet girl and a good student, embroiled in the drama of the typical teenager. She had quarreled with her boyfriend on Friday, October 17, but did not sit home crying that night. She joined her friends for pizza, advising her parents not to expect her home till midnight.

At some point that evening, she decided to visit her boyfriend and asked a friend to drop her off near his home. He and his parents, however, reported that she never arrived.

A witness spotted a young girl matching Emily's description walking on a deserted street in the early morning hours of Saturday. Someone else in the area heard moaning in the alley behind their house and later discovered a bloody dollar bill and a wig. Though police suspected that the moaning was connected to Emily, the clues made little sense.

Emily was found strangled in a field on Saturday afternoon.

"The case has many loose ends," said Richard. "It was never solved."

Poor Emily still wanders in the field where her body was found. Today, Richard Crowe explained, it is the site of the new Morton College, built in the 1970s.

"The new college was not yet finished when her ghost was spotted," he said.

A man was working on the roof when he was startled to see a teenager in white walking along the edge. He called to her, and she stepped out into the air and vanished. "When he ran to the edge and looked down, there was no one there," said Richard.

Since that day, the troubled spirit occasionally appears on the roof. She is also known to play with the elevator, slam doors, and toss stones.

If Emily had not been murdered, she would be fifty-five years old and probably a grandmother by now. But the breath was cruelly snatched from her lungs by a monster. Maybe her killer is still alive and feels no guilt, and that is why the spirit of Emily cannot rest.

"Perhaps the solution to her murder will free her," said Richard.

We don't know if the detectives harvested and saved DNA from the homicide. If they did, recent scientific breakthroughs could soon put detectives on the heels of the killer. His days may be numbered, and Emily could finally graduate to a peaceful plane.

Ghosts in the News

Monster in Our Midst

THE SITE OF A HORRIFIC unsolved murder in Keddie, California, is believed to be haunted, according to a June 10, 2001, article in the *San Francisco Gate*.

Keddie Resort, founded in 1910, was once a placid vacation spot where visitors could rent one of thirty-three rustic cabins or a room in the lodge, reported writer Kevin Fagan. People drove hundreds of miles to the northern Sierra Mountains resort to explore the pristine wooded trails and dine at the Keddie Lodge Restaurant, which was packed nightly as customers lined up to eat wild game and sip fine wine.

Everything changed on April 11, 1981, when four people were brutally tortured and murdered in Cabin 28. Thirty-six-year-old Glenna Sharp; her son, fifteen-year-old John Sharp; and his friend seventeen-year-old Dana Wingate were bound and killed.

Sheila Sharp, fourteen, had spent the night at a friend's, and the poor girl discovered her loved ones in the carnage. Her two younger brothers and their friend who was spending the night were unharmed, but her thirteen-year-old sister, Tina, was missing. Tina's skull was discovered three years later by a bottle digger.

With the public too frightened to visit, the resort "rotted into a refuge for squatters and hobos," wrote Kevin Fagan. He also reported that the campground was being restored and would soon reopen. The "Murder House," however, was a dark reminder.

Its windows covered with plywood, and its doors nailed shut, it was a site so filled with evil that even seasoned detectives did not like to step inside. The many curious neighborhood kids and homeless people seeking shelter who have broken into Cabin 28 have all ended up fleeing in terror.

While some locals were skeptical of the idea that the place is haunted, others told Fagan that they had seen eerie floating figures; had heard footsteps, doors slamming, and moans in the empty house; and had witnessed objects that inexplicably materialized there.

Frustrated detectives continue to work the very sad cold case that left so many mourning and so few clues.

two

Within the Shadows

The old beggar woman sometimes drew pitiful stares from the passersby. Other times, people gazed at her with self-righteous scorn. Their eyes said that they thought she was as low as a piece of manure stuck to the bottom of their shoes. They could not see that the ragged woman was more like they were than they could have imagined; that she had been born to a respectable family and had once dreamed of being a wife and mother.

They did not want to recognize the human bond. The shabby figure was not only a shameful sight, but she would soon become as all who are born will eventually be: dead.

Maybe something in her eyes made them shiver as they quickened their stride to pass her on the cobblestone street. If they looked too long, they might just recognize the fatal likeness. One day they, too, would be united with her in death.

There is something about Morrill Hall that makes the skin creep. Perhaps it is the fact that it is one of oldest buildings on the University of Maryland campus and exudes the spooky ambience typical of historic structures. Or maybe it is the ghosts that peek out of the windows at night.

Students have reported sudden flashes of light in the dark windows, followed by the appearance of an apparition. Framed in the window, the face gazes out. As one brave student approached the window, the image quickly faded.

Built in 1898, Morrill Hall was the only structure to survive with all its walls intact when a Thanksgiving Day fire roared through the campus in 1912.

In recent years, workers were installing an air conditioner in Morrill Hall when an overpowering burning odor pervaded the place. Firefighters were called to investigate and concluded that when the drills bored into the walls, they had released vestiges of fumes and ashes from the long-ago blaze.

Those who have experienced phenomena there wonder what else was released.

In October 2004 interviews with the student newspaper, the *Diamond Back*, university staff with offices in Morrill Hall offered varied perspectives on the ghost tales associated with the building. While Charles Cadwell told reporter Caitlin Evans that the odd noises heard there were only squirrels and the wind, June Tuman argued, "There were certain sounds upstairs that sounded like more than the wind and more than squirrels. . . ."

June Tuman admitted that she no longer heard the distinctive footsteps emanating from overhead, because she no longer stayed late. She did not, however, clarify if her schedule change was due to fear or convenience.

A popular Halloween subject among student reporters, Morrill Hall has been written about frequently. And many of the young writers point out a possible connection between the ghosts and a grisly discovery there. Nearly a century ago, the building was used by medical students who dissected cadavers. Everyone was shocked when, years later, someone found human remains there. Workers discovered the parts, long forgotten beneath a sink.

Do the ghosts on campus belong to those who were so carelessly discarded by sloppy medical students years ago?

Maybe.

This writer suspects at least one of the ghosts belongs to a troubled woman who ghost investigators have not yet named. They are likely not even aware of her, for her appalling story unfolded before most of our grandparents were born. She, too, has the roots of her torment planted in the old medical school.

Emily Brown was born around 1826 and grew up to be a genius with the sewing needle. The daughter of a hotel owner in Easton, Maryland, her young life was comfortable and probably happy. Somehow, the decades slipped by, and she did not fulfill the destiny of women in that era. She never married. She never had a child.

The middle-aged spinster sought comfort in opium and alcohol. She roomed with a family on Pig Alley in Baltimore and was known on the street as "Beggar Brown."

On the morning of December 10, 1886, she ate breakfast with another boarder in the home. No one knows if Emily noticed Anderson Perry scrutinizing her from across the table. No one knows if she felt his eyes, summing her up, calculating the fortune he hoped she would bring him.

Anderson was a custodian at the nearby University of Maryland's School of Medicine. He had a get-rich scheme. Students of the medical school needed cadavers to dissect. They needed them so badly that the school paid fifteen dollars for each body brought to them.

That sounded good to John Thomas Ross and Albert Hawkins. At Anderson's urging, they slipped into the Pig Alley house and attacked sixty-year-old Emily Brown. They struck her over the head with a brick and stabbed her in the chest. She was packed into a sack, stuffed in a wheelbarrow, and taken straight to the door of the school's dissection room. Anderson Perry was waiting there, and the three congratulated themselves as they split the cash.

Five dollars for a day's work was good pay in 1886. Unfortunately for the killers, the brutal manner of their victim's death raised suspicions, and the police were called.

Baltimore citizens were shocked by the headline in the *Baltimore Sun*, the next day: Burking in Baltimore. The article spoke of the practice, which originated with serial killer William Burke in the 1820s. The onetime Irish grave robber saw a chance for fast cash by murdering people instead of unearthing those who had died of natural causes. He killed approximately thirty people in Edinburgh, Scotland, and sold them for dissection.

Some folks in Baltimore were so rattled by the "Baltimore Burking" that they refused to go near the medical school for fear they would be killed for dissection. The case accelerated the passing of laws banning payment for cadavers.

As for the killers, Anderson Perry and Albert Hawkins escaped prosecution. John Thomas Ross was convicted. He was hanged in the summer of 1887.

In a kind of poetic justice, many years later, Anderson Perry's body was found among the dissection cadavers after a campus fire. Though he had apparently died of natural causes, he was penniless.

It may be the ghost of Emily Brown who students have spied peeking from the windows of empty buildings at night. To Emily, it may still be 1886, and she could be baffled by the changing terrain. Her soul might seek refuge in the campus's oldest structures, as she searches for something familiar.

Poor Emily will never find her way back to Pig Alley, for the old bumpy street is long gone, replaced by a smooth wide road that runs past the ballpark.

While Emily is a definite candidate for a University of Maryland ghost, others whose bodies were dissected there may also be bound to the campus. Maybe the smiling child in the big bonnet and the yellow dress served medical science there.

Or maybe she was a farm girl who lived and died in the area before the school was established.

The grinning apparition has been witnessed by folks in the campus's Rossborough Inn. One employee who worked in the 1798 brick building saw the little specter after a gust blew the window open. He peered out and saw the disembodied face smiling at him. When she next appeared, some time later, he could also see her yellow dress and apron.

Because he had kept the vision to himself, he knew he hadn't been seeing things when another employee validated his sighting. He confided that he had seen a ghost and also described a smiling girl in a yellow dress.

Marie Mount is another spirit believed to be tied to the school. The first dean of home economics was said to be so attached to the college that she wished to stay forever.

Students in the Marie Mount Hall have reported the materialization of her spirit. Others attribute the inexplicable sound of the piano playing to her phantom fingers dancing over the ivories. It happens, they say, on stormy days. When the sky is knitted with thick gray clouds, rain slashes the windows, and the rumble of thunder rolls over the roof, Marie Mount makes music.

Does the ghost of Marie Mount haunt the University of Maryland campus? (1932 yearbook)

While her life did not end violently, there are, sadly, no shortages of tragic deaths at the old campus, and therefore, no shortage of ghosts. Perhaps closest to the campus heart, is the ghost of another woman who was the university's very own. Nearly half a century has past since her unjust death. The students still talk about her, and it is common knowledge that she inhabits the sorority house she helped establish.

᪥

When you gaze at the friendly face of Alma Preinkert in the university's old yearbooks, the innocence is striking. Her expression is friendly and expectant, as if she believes the future is full of good things.

The longtime registrar at the University of Maryland was popular with the students. Indeed, she must have empathized with them, as she, too, had attended the university, where she earned a master's degree.

The old photos show no sign of a premonition of doom. And that is probably best. Even when she did sense danger near, there was nothing she could do about it. Or was there?

Alma Preinkert smiles from the yearbook of the University of Maryland. (1932 yearbook)

If Alma Preinkert could say one thing to students today, it may very well be, "*Trust your gut. If you have a feeling that something is not right, listen to your instincts before it is too late.*"

Indeed, countless women with close brushes with killers have confided that they avoided tragedy, because they trusted their first inkling that something was not right.

On the last night of her life, Alma knew something was not right.

It was February 28, 1954, and she and her sister, Margaret Heine, had played bridge with friends and returned to their adjacent houses in Washington, D.C., at about one a.m. Alma, fifty-eight, told Margaret of her premonition. They said goodnight, and Alma went into the house she shared with her other sister, Alvina.

Did Alma wonder if it was not safe to stay in her home that night, or did she dismiss her uneasy feelings as she slipped beneath her blankets?

We will never know, for as she slumbered, evil lurked outside her home. A burglar found a ladder in a nearby yard, placed it against Alma's yellow clapboard house, and climbed to her second-story window.

Only an hour had passed since Alma had shared her premonition with her sister. Now, she awoke to see a man rummaging through her dresser drawers. Caught in the act, he stabbed the terrified woman. The sounds of her screams brought Alvina running to help, and she, too, was knifed. Alvina survived but Alma died.

Police soon swarmed the house and found just one small clue. It was a gold tie clasp, discovered in Alma's room.

Detectives canvassed the neighborhood, interviewing over five hundred people. Neighbors who had heard the frantic screams admitted that they had not rushed to help, because they figured the commotion was "just an alley fight."

Classes were suspended for Alma's funeral. Students crowded the Memorial Chapel to mourn "Miss Preink," the woman who had always found time to listen. Her funeral was so packed that some students were forced to stand outside in a rainstorm as they paid their respects.

Alma's killer has yet to be named. Her unsolved murder is just one more in a staggering stack of cold cases that result in earthbound souls. And it is Alma, students whisper, who is responsible for the perplexing things that happen in a particular sorority house.

Alma had helped to establish the Maryland chapter of the Kappa Delta Sorority on campus. It's only natural that she has an attachment to the place, say some girls who have resided there. She is a friendly spirit, and most residents enjoy the novelty of living in a haunted house.

When an item is mysteriously misplaced, Alma is playfully scolded. The creaking floors, the sudden chills, and the darting shadows are all attributed to her.

And maybe it was Alma who invited some old friends over for a party one summer day when the sorority house was closed. Witnesses swore they saw girls in white dresses dancing on the porch when the house was deserted.

If the theory that spirits can take the form of themselves at any age is true, than Alma may have been among the frolicking girls. She could have materialized as she was in an innocent time, when she, too, was a student with stars in her eyes. While her fate was nothing to celebrate, there was nothing to stop her from celebrating the past.

Big **Moose** Murder

Ever since she was a little girl, Lynda Lee Macken was fascinated by the subject of ghosts. "But I never ever wanted to see one," said the Forked River, New Jersey, author who admitted that the idea terrified her.

By the time she had reached thirty without a single sighting, she figured that she would never see a ghost. And she certainly was not looking for one on the dark night she unwittingly visited a murder site and a ghost found her.

The leading cause of death for pregnant women is not a medical ailment. It is not childbirth, and it is not an accident. It is murder, usually committed by the victim's boyfriend or husband.

When Grace Brown found herself unwed and with child, it was a disgraceful situation. In today's American culture, folks barely blink an eye when an unwed woman gives birth. But Grace became pregnant in 1906, when women didn't vote, didn't wear slacks, and certainly did not have babies before marriage without causing a stir.

Men in that era may have felt even more trapped by an unwanted pregnancy than they do today. Chances are, quite a few of them got away with murder. Chester Gillette was not one of them.

Chester Gillette met Grace Brown at his uncle's skirt factory in Cortland, New York. It was 1905, and he found himself attracted to the pretty farm girl. The coworkers dated on the sly, and before long she had unwelcome news for him. She was carrying his baby.

Did he promise to marry her?

The letters she sent him, pleading with him to be true to his word, indicated that he had. We can only imagine the hope she felt when it looked as if they were going to be wed, and together boarded a train headed for the Adirondacks, the pristine mountainous region in northern New York. As the rolling green hills flashed past the windows, did Grace and Chester talk about the future, perhaps discussing names for the baby?

The soft rumble of the train in motion must have had a relaxing effect, and Grace likely daydreamed about her future throughout the trip. By winter, she would have a sweet baby in her arms, and the handsome husband by her side would adore their child.

Grace was not privy to the thoughts in Chester's head. While she contemplated her new life, he was planning her death.

They stayed at the Glenmore Hotel on Big Moose Lake, and Chester suggested they rent a rowboat. Grace could not swim, but she had her fiancé to protect her. The romantic scenario sounds like something in a Monet painting. The lazy summer afternoon. The deep lake, reflecting shades of green. Chester, his muscles flexing with each pull of the oars, and Grace, her delicate fingers trailing in the water.

No one knows the exact moment when the tranquil scene changed, but by evening, the lifeless body of Grace was resting on the bottom of the lake, her long hair waving with each ripple. Soon after the body was discovered, Chester was fingered as a suspect.

The joyful winter that Grace had imagined would never arrive. Instead, November saw the beginning of the murder trial for the man she had loved. It was a feeding frenzy for reporters, who flocked to the courtroom for the scandalous details the public waited to hear. Chester swore that he had not killed Grace. It was suicide, he insisted. The troubled woman had leapt from the boat and intentionally drowned herself.

But the smoking gun in this case was a bloody tennis racket, found hidden in the shrubs beside the lake. Prosecutors maintained that Chester had struck his unsuspecting victim on the head before dumping her in the water. A jury found Chester Gillette guilty of first-degree murder and sentenced him to death. He was strapped to the death chair and electrocuted on March 30, 1908.

The murder inspired books and movies, including the book and film *An American Tragedy* and the movie *A Place in the Sun*.

If Lynda Lee Macken had ever seen the old movies, she did not connect them with the wilderness retreat to which she and her best friend, Bridgett, had traveled. They had chosen Big Moose Lake, because it was the area where a favorite author had built a cabin.

"We had no idea there had been a murder there," she said. They checked into Covewood Lodge and chose a rustic cabin near the lake. "We spent a day canoeing," said Lynda. "The water was crystal clear, and you could see all the way to the bottom."

The friends were awed by the wildlife as they watched black bears wandering in the distance on the edge of the ancient forest. "Yet, I felt uneasy from the moment we arrived," confided Lynda. She was uncharacteristically jumpy. She found herself afraid to look out the windows at night when darkness swallowed their cabin. "I slept with the lights on," she said.

She didn't know what to make of it when the fresh batteries in her flashlight, camera, and clock were suddenly and inexplicably dead. "That was before I knew anything about ghosts, so I didn't realize that they drain batteries," she said.

She was headed to the gazebo by the lakeside when the batteries in her flashlight died. The moonless night offered no light, and the darkness was as black as ink. She stumbled back to the cabin and asked Bridgett to grab her flashlight and join her. As they sat in the gazebo, the low, eerie calls of the loons filled the night. "I was trying to tell Bridgett something, and she kept interrupting," remembered Lynda. "I was getting really annoyed, because she kept pointing to the mist on the lake."

"Look!" said Bridgett. "The mist is headed this way. Oh, look! It's stopping in front of that cabin!" She suddenly gasped. "Oh, my God! Look! It's a ghost!"

Lynda turned her head to see the distinct form of a lovely woman floating above the water. Though translucent, the figure was vividly detailed. She did not seem to notice her awed observers. Instead, she stared at the cabin as Lynda memorized every detail of the ethereal creature's profile. She noted she wore a Gibson girl blouse with a high neck. She saw that the ghost had hands, and that her hair hung loose. "I looked for her feet, but she didn't have any," said Lynda. "Her legs trailed off into the mist."

Though not frightened, Lynda felt an overpowering grief wash over her. "I had such a feeling of sadness," she said. "One that I have never felt again."

As the women watched, the spirit faded back into the night.

The next day they began to ask questions, and Lynda learned of the long-ago murder. "Grace was found in the deepest part of the lake, known as Punky Bay," said Lynda. "That was the spot where the mist originated."

The encounter had such a profound effect on Lynda Lee Macken that it inspired her to pen the first of her fourteen nonfiction books on East Coast hauntings. Since she published *Adirondack Ghosts*, others have come forward to say that they, too, have encountered the spirit of Big Moose Lake.

From sightings of ghosts from the windows of the lakeside hotels, to the distinct image of the beautiful specter seen through a video lens, the encounters with the poor soul continue.

Grace Brown lost so much a century ago. She lost the love she thought she had, the baby she longed to hold, and a future that should have been happy.

By the time Lynda Lee Macken told Grace's story, there was little she could do to help the murdered woman, but perhaps having someone to empathize with her was help enough.

To read more about Adirondack ghosts, consult Lynda's Web site at: *www.lyndaleemacken.com*

Where the Dead Can't Sleep

Get out a globe, close your eyes, and spin. No matter where it stops, you are sure to be staring at a spot near a haunted location where the restless wraiths wrought from murder roam.

Here are a few places where victims' ghosts are encountered:

Midnight Visitor

Gadsby's Tavern Museum in historic Alexandria, Virginia, is haunted by a dentist whose killer got away with murder. According to guides who lead the Ghosts and Graveyards Tours, the structure in Old Town was once known as Wise's Tavern and had a basement apartment where tenants did not stay long. Plagued with terrible nightmares and ghostly visits, the residents hurriedly packed and moved. One woman awoke to see the apartment engulfed in flames, but the scene soon faded. She had witnessed not a real fire, but a reenactment of the long-ago burning of a murder victim. Another tenant was shocked to see a specter in her rocking chair. The apparition had a knife sticking from his eye.

The ghostly visits finally made sense when charred remains and a rusted dagger were found in a pit beneath the apartment. Detectives believed the remains belonged to a dentist who had vanished from the tavern years before. The murdered man's spirit may have been trying to alert someone to his predicament by reenacting his death.

GADSBY'S TAVERN MUSUEM
134 North Royal Street
Alexandria, VA 22314
(703) 838-4242

Ghost on the Green

In Victoria, British Columbia, a golf course is said to be haunted by the troubled spirit of Doris Gravlin. Locals say that the victim of a murder-suicide takes many forms as she stalks the Victoria Golf Course. She is reportedly most frequently seen at night during the month of March. Some witness a misty figure, while others are startled by a hovering bright ball of light.

Many claim to have seen the apparition of Doris, floating along in a long white wedding gown. Others report that the murdered woman's ghost runs into the road and has even tried to climb into cars.

Strangled by her husband, Victor, in the 1930s and buried in a sand trap, Doris is believed to be searching for justice. Perhaps she does not realize that her husband took his own life, too. If he is serving time for his crime, it is not in this world.

The Victoria Golf Course is located on Gonzales Point and overlooks Oak Bay in Victoria, B.C.

Permanent Guest

Does the disgruntled ghost of a murdered man haunt the Stagecoach Inn Museum in Newbury Park, California?

Yes. No. Maybe.

It depends on whom you ask. While the museum's Web site mentions the legend, it takes a skeptical tone. Others insist the place is home to many spirits.

Years ago, renowned psychic Sybil Leek claimed to make contact with the spirit of victim Pierre Duvon, supposedly killed in 1885 when the site was occupied by the Grand Union Hotel.

If Pierre is there, he is not alone. Some say they have encountered the specter of a tall woman and have heard the voice a small boy. Legend has it that the child disappeared while staying in the hotel in the late 1800s.

Some say he wandered off and was lost in the wilderness. Others believe he was kidnapped and killed.

THE STAGECOACH INN MUSEUM

51 Ventu Park Road

Newbury Park, CA 91320

(805) 498-9441

Web site: *www.stagecoachmuseum.org*

Dressed to Kill

When the grand jury ruled that the demise of a famous actress was a suicide, many believed they had made a mistake. And others insisted that it was the injustice of that decision that brought the victim back from the dead.

Thelma Todd immediately won fans when she made her first film in 1926. Nine years and forty movies later, the blond bombshell was decidedly famous. Fans adored her in her funny roles in the Marx Brothers' movies, *Monkey Business* and *Horse Feathers*.

When she opened her own restaurant, Thelma Todd's Sidewalk Café in Pacific Palisades, California, people visited as much for the brush with fame as for the food.

The movie star resided in the swanky apartment upstairs and, to outsiders, it seemed to be an ideal life. Yet Thelma had troubles. In 1935, friends said she was depressed. She had endured a tumultuous marriage and divorce and was teetering toward bankruptcy. Was it enough for her to take drastic measures?

On December 16, 1935, Thelma's body was discovered in her 1934 convertible, her beautiful face resting on the steering wheel. The car had become a death tool, the lethal carbon monoxide snatching her breath away. Clad in a mink coat, mauve and silver evening gown, and shimmering jewelry, Thelma was dressed to kill. But did she kill herself?

The mystery of Thelma's death still captures the imaginations of backseat detectives, who pick at the decades-old puzzle as they try to make the pieces fit. At this late date, the nature of Thelma's true fate will likely never be known.

Today, the building that houses Thelma's old café is home to Paulist Productions, a company dedicated to making religious films.

Thelma Todd is still seen.

The ghost of the glamorous movie star is said to materialize on the outside steps, which once connected her apartment to her café. The specter moves down the stairs before vanishing.

Visitors to the garage where Thelma died sometimes get a taste of her last moments. Witnesses insist that an inexplicable, overpowering odor of carbon monoxide has sent them running from the area. It is almost as if Thelma's ghost is sharing her last horrible experience in an effort to make others understand.

THELMA TODD'S SIDEWALK CAFÉ

once occupied the first floor of a building at:

17575 Pacific Coast Highway

Pacific Palisades, CA

It's the Principal

Students of the Michelago Primary School in Australia have more to fear than pop quizzes if they believe the stories of the specter who haunts their halls. Legend has it that the school's principal was murdered in the late nineteenth century. His wife was responsible for his demise but was declared insane.

When windows, which normally glide open easily, become inexplicably stuck, the ghost of the slain principal is blamed. Objects are moved about during the night, and someone leaves items scattered about the floor.

The ghostly principal is a restless spirit who may be unaware that he is dead.

The Michelago Primary School is located in Michelago, New South Wales, Australia.

Curtain Call

In Paris, Texas, about a hundred miles northeast of Dallas, residents say that the ghost of a murdered woman haunts the Plaza Theatre. This historic landmark opened its doors in 1926 and awed patrons with its plush interior, complete with a pipe organ, orchestra pit, and ornate foyer.

Soon after the grand opening, a young woman sat in the balcony, enjoying a Rudolph Valentino flick, when someone crept up on her.

Annabelle may have been so entranced with the larger-than-life figures on the movie screen that she did not sense the evil near her. She was attacked and strangled. According to lore, the killer escaped detection.

Annabelle forever wanders the theater, which is today the home of the Paris Community Theatre. Cast and crew report frequent paranormal activity.

Annabelle keeps everyone on their toes by borrowing and moving items. And some report that when her eerie shriek echoes through the building, it turns their blood to ice.

Poor Annabelle may not realize that it is too late to scream for help.

PLAZA THEATRE
102 Downtown Plaza
Paris, TX 75460
(903) 784-0259

In Death They Don't Part

Star-crossed lovers inhabit the Double Eagle Restaurant in Mesilla, New Mexico. They may be dead, but they are still in love.

Employees and customers have witnessed mugs gliding across the tables as if invisible hands were guiding them, heard the sound of disembodied voices, and been startled by the ethereal woman who appears outside the kitchen door.

What is the cause of this paranormal activity?

Locals whisper that it is the ghosts of teenage Armando Maese and his love, Inez. A century before the restaurant opened, the building was a stately mansion and home to the wealthy Maese family. According to legend, the snobbish Carlota Maese grew suspicious when she saw that her son noticed the lovely teenaged maid. Armando's eyes followed Inez as she did her chores. Her gleaming black hair fell to her waist, and he saw a spark in her eyes as she smiled shyly at him.

When love blossomed, the Maeses' other servants tried to hide the fact from Carlota for they knew she would not be pleased. Indeed she was not.

She was enraged. This was not the union she had planned for her son.

When she caught the young lovers in a compromising situation, she flew at them with a pair of scissors, intent on ripping into the maid's flesh. Armando jumped in front of Inez to protect her. His angry mother accidentally stabbed him.

The couple bled to death in each other's arms.

Some believe that the tragic lovers' feelings were so powerful that they still linger in the place they met. When the empty chairs move at the cozy corner table, waitresses wonder if it is the young couple on a date.

DOUBLE EAGLE RESTAURANT

2355 Calle De Guadalupe

Mesilla, NM 88046

(505) 523-6700

www.double-eagle-mesilla.com

Appetite for Murder

When a young boy suddenly appears near the stove in the Queensberry House in Edinburgh, Scotland, stunned witnesses know they
have glimpsed the victim of a shocking tragedy. The servant boy found
himself in an unfortunate predicament when he was confronted in the
kitchen by a very crazy and very hungry James Douglas.

It was 1707, and James, oldest son of the Duke of Queensberry,
escaped from his quarters and wandered into the kitchen. The servant
boy was alone in the house. Everyone else was out, swept up in the
excitement of the Treaty of the Union.

The disturbed youth wrestled with the terrified servant and managed to mount him on a spit and roast him alive. James was enjoying
his snack when the other servants returned to the shocking scenario.

The Queensberry House is now part of the Scottish Parliament
complex. The 1686 house retains the infamous stove, and many have
reported the inexplicable scent of cooking meat. Sightings of the 300-
year-old ghost continue to this day.

Holyrood Road
On the Canongate in Edinburgh

𝕲𝖍𝖔𝖘𝖙𝖘 𝖎𝖓 𝖙𝖍𝖊 𝕹𝖊𝖜𝖘

Business as Usual

THE ROBBERY VICTIM killed in his store in Sundance, Wyoming, is still tending to business, according to the October 31, 2005, issue of the *Casper Star Tribune*.

Paul Sharp operated his hardware store for thirty-three years until the morning of October 14, 1983, when he was brutally murdered. Paul's widow, Ethel, who kept the business going for fifteen years after the tragedy, was often heard to say that she never felt alone in the store.

When Rocky Courchaine turned the store into a western gift and antique shop where he makes his own jewelry, he too, soon realized he was not alone. He told reporter Sean Conneely that late one night he looked up to see someone walking through the store. "I had left the front door unlocked," he said. "So I figured someone had just wandered in."

When he searched the building, however, he discovered he was alone. He locked the front door and then witnessed a phantom figure walking through the store several more times before the night was over.

The specter continued to make appearances, and eventually Rocky was able to size him up long enough to recognize him. It was the spirit of Paul Sharp, dressed in his typical attire of dark pants and white shirt. Rocky also noted that the ghost always cut the same path through the store—from the office to the spot where the register sat for fifty years.

The encounters, he admitted, changed him from a skeptic to a believer.

three

The Third Eye

"I can't get his face out of my mind," the girl told me. "I saw him so clearly. He murdered someone."

I had just finished giving a ghost talk at the library, and the twelve-year-old girl was troubled, as she described the recurring scenario in her dreams. "It's near a baseball field, and there is a body in the Dumpster," she continued. "It is the same every time I dream it."

In each dream, the girl saw the victim's long hair rippling in the wind but could not see her face. She had never seen the man in real life, did not recognize the baseball field, and had no idea of the identity of the victim.

Yet she felt that she was experiencing something that had actually happened or was going to happen. If there was something she could do to help, she wanted to do it. But what could she possibly do with the information? The nightmares disturbed her.

I told her that she may very well be psychic and could be having visions, and that she had choices. She could either work to develop her gift, or she could pray that the visions would stop.

While psychic talent is not unusual, it can be a burden, especially if the medium tunes in to violence. Throughout my life, I have had psychic dreams, and when I was young, they disturbed me. Some were just strange.

For instance, I once had a dream about a funny man doing an odd dance. Suddenly his hair caught on fire. I woke up and turned on the radio, only to hear that Michael Jackson's hair had caught fire while he was dancing as he filmed a Pepsi commercial.

Other times, the things I saw in my dreams were so horrible that they haunted me throughout the day. I could not discern what was a vision and what was just a nightmare. I prayed that the dreams would stop and that God would take away my premonitions. It worked. For a few years, the dreams stopped, and they did not return until I was able to emotionally handle it.

I wished I could do more for the troubled twelve-year-old who could not banish the visions of homicide. That night, I spent hours on the Web, trying to find a scenario that matched what the young girl had described. It was a frustrating task with no definitive results. I knew there was little I could do for the girl with the visions or the possible victims of a monster.

If it is difficult for a twelve-year-old girl to psychically connect with the horrors of homicide, imagine how hard it is for a four-year-old!

I found one such child in San Antonio, Texas, after reading a post on psychic Da Juana Byrd's Web site.

"My four-year-old sees ghosts," the mother wrote. She described the invisible playmate the little girl had recently acquired. The boy, said the child, was named Alex, and he had been murdered.

San Antonio paranormal investigator Martin Leal and I met with the mother and her three small children in a Texas park where the boy said he had been murdered.

While I normally use real names, I will give the family pseudonyms here, because I do not want to put them in danger. If indeed a boy was killed, a murderer roams free. Chances are, the killer will never read this book, but I choose not to take any chances.

The trouble began shortly after the Everson family moved into a new apartment in San Antonio. Their daughter, Kelsey, who had always slept well, suddenly began having nightmares.

"She would wake up, kicking and screaming," said her mother,

Theresa Everson. "By the time my husband and I could wake her up, she had no memories of her dreams."

The description of the episodes sounded like a sleep disturbance known as "night terrors." Many children are afflicted with this, particularly around ages three and four. While adults also suffer from the sleep disorder, it is most common in children. Though night terrors do not fall into the paranormal category, I was not ready to dismiss the child's experiences.

Kelsey told her mother that a little boy, covered in blood, visited her nightly. She claimed that he hit her in the back with an object. His name was Alex.

Theresa phoned a psychic friend, Cathy, who agreed to visit their apartment. Unaware of the details of Kelsey's experiences, Cathy, too, picked up on the ghost of a little boy.

Cathy described the ghost as about six years old, with short brown hair. He was covered in blood. "He told me that he was murdered by his mother's boyfriend in a San Antonio park," she said.

The family had picnicked in the park with the mother's boyfriend's coworkers. As they got ready to leave, the boyfriend told Alex to pick up his toys. When the child did not move fast enough, the man became enraged. He beat the boy to death and buried him in an old well.

The child's pregnant mother did nothing to help him.

The ghost, Cathy said, told her that a reporter from the *San Antonio Morning News* had visited his mother to inquire about the missing child's whereabouts. Apparently, nothing came of the reporter's investigation.

Cathy also claimed that the murdered spirit told her that he had not meant to hurt Kelsey when he had hit her. "I was just trying to show her what would happen if she was bad," the dead boy said. "Adults are bad people."

Shortly after Cathy's visit, the family headed out for a day at Espada Park. Kelsey curled up in the backseat and refused to get out of the car. "Alex is scared," she said. "This is where it happened."

Had Kelsey overheard her parents discussing Cathy's encounter? Had the power of suggestion wreaked havoc on the little girl's imagination?

The parents may have been unwittingly feeding their daughter's fears.

Yet, Kelsey had drawn pictures of the park beforehand. She drew pictures of the turtles Alex had played with in the park.

"I found out that at one time there were turtles at Espada Park. But they have not been seen in years," said Theresa, who believes that Alex was killed at the park at least a decade before.

It was a sweltering day when Martin Leal and I gathered around the old well in the woods with Theresa's children. Kelsey seemed hesitant as she gazed into the well, which was now filled with dirt and litter.

Was a little boy really buried there?

Martin got out his electromagnetic field detector, a tool that picks up on anomalies in the environment that many believe to be indicative of ghosts. He aimed at the well and the places where Kelsey said the ghost was. Nothing out of the ordinary registered.

I gently asked Kelsey about Alex.

Her young face clouded as she told me, "His daddy got him dead."

The weapon? A tire iron.

According to Theresa, her daughter had drawn a picture of a tire iron and claimed that the man had used it to hurt Alex. She insisted that her daughter was not aware of Cathy's interaction with the boy's spirit, and that the child had drawn the pictures with no prompting.

I cannot say for certain that a boy named Alex was murdered in San Antonio. But if he was, perhaps this story will ring a bell with someone who is familiar with his story, and we can help a lost child find his way to the light.

For the unprepared, a visit from a ghost can be a disturbing experience. Yet, even those who are prepared and make a practice of contacting spirits sometimes find that the encounters are more than they can stand.

The psychics in the following story will never forget the horror they felt while visiting a murder site.

Waking the Dead

Slay utterly old and young, both maids, and little children . . .

Ezekiel 9:6 (KJV)

Brenda Marble, of Harrisonville, Missouri, cannot explain the lure of a simple Iowa farmhouse. It drew her to it, again and again. Each time she visited, she swore it would be the last. Yet, it seemed there was a message that she was chosen to tell the world. The house would not let her go until she and her friends deciphered that message and passed it along.

It should have been a lovely spring day filled with the sounds of birds singing and children laughing. But June 10, 1912, in Villisca, Iowa, was the darkest day in the history of the town.

The first inkling that something was wrong at the Moore house came when Mary Peckman peered down the street and noticed that her neighbors were not up and about. She grew more alarmed when she investigated and found the house tightly closed with all the shades drawn over the windows.

Worried, she spread the word, and before long, the brother of Joe Moore showed up and used his spare key to enter the home.

He stepped into a nightmare. The usually lively home was too quiet and washed in darkness. Every window and mirror in the home was covered with blankets or clothing. As his eyes adjusted, he did not want to believe what he saw.

Everyone was dead.

Someone had crept into the house and killed all the occupants with an axe. Joe, forty-three; Sarah, thirty-eight; Herman, eleven; Catherine, ten; Boyd, seven; and Paul, five; made up the entire Moore family.

The children's friends Lena and Ina Stillinger, ages twelve and eight, had been spending the night, and they, too, were dead.

A crowd soon gathered outside the death house, and the curious pushed their way into the home, gawking at the mutilated bodies and trampling over evidence. The crime scene was destroyed.

Over the next years, investigators focused on three suspects. There was the Reverend Lyn George Jacklin Kelly, a minister who had been visiting the town the night of the murders.

Mentally unstable, at one point he confessed to the killings, saying he was inspired by a sermon he was working on, taken from the book of Ezekiel in the Bible, which has a verse that begins, "Slay utterly old and young . . ."

As any seasoned detective knows, compulsive confessors crawl out of the woodwork to admit to crimes they did not commit. In addition, it appeared that the reverend may have been pressured to confess.

Then there was Frank Jones, a rich and powerful rival of Joe Moore's. Each owned a hardware store, and the competition had grown bitter.

William Mansfield also was investigated. He was a suspect in the axe murder of his wife, daughter, and in-laws in Blue Island, Illinois. His modus operandi was similar to that of the Villisca killer.

The convoluted case and its investigation inspired books and documentaries. Perhaps if the case had been solved, there would not be such interest in it today.

Apparently residents of Villisca were not altogether repelled by the history of the house. When a documentary maker interviewed an elderly woman whose family had lived there after the murder, she smiled as she recalled her childhood sleeping in the blood-splattered room.

Though no one interviewed on the documentary mentioned ethereal encounters, it may simply be that they were not sensitive enough to sense the spirits in the home.

Or it could be that new owners woke the spirits from a daze.

When Darwin and Martha Linn purchased the old house, they restored it to resemble the grisly day in 1912. Crime buffs flock there to take the tours.

Like a dial on a radio, the ambience was set to pick up signals from beyond.

When people began to notice ghostly stirrings in the house, a small but determined investigative group from Missouri got on the case. Six members of the Miller Paranormal Research team traveled to Villisca. Brenda Marble, Dee Ann Tripses, Jerry Miller, Kathy Burhart, and psychics Joyce Morgan and Misty Maeder entered the historic murder site in August 2003, equipped with their electronic detection tools and their keen sixth sense.

The stage was set to draw visitors to the past, Brenda noted, as she inhaled the heavy odor of the kerosene lamps. Those with imagination could find themselves back in the era of the brutal night. Add intuition to that, and it may be more than you bargained for.

Joyce Morgan was so tuned into the horror, that she was overcome with emotion on her first visit, as disturbing images of the children invaded her senses. She opted to leave the house.

The rest of the team spent the night, one they will never forget.

It was two a.m., possibly the exact hour that the mass murder occurred, when the spirits came alive.

Investigators theorized that the killer went into action as the train roared through town, the scream of its whistle drowning out the screams of his victims.

When the whistle sounded the first night that the Miller team visited, it seemed to literally wake the dead. Misty, Dee Ann, and Brenda watched in astonishment as a fog moved through the upstairs rooms of the old farmhouse.

It began in the parents' room and settled in the children's room. "It was as if the whole room went out of focus," Brenda told me.

Through her third eye, psychic Misty Maeder then saw a reenactment of the attacks on the children.

The train passed, and the world became still.

"It was so quiet," Brenda told me. "There were no clocks ticking, and it was not raining. It was eerily silent."

And then came a noise that made the hair on the backs of their necks rise. All three women heard the distinctive sound of dripping. It came from the direction of one of the girls' beds.

It was the sound of blood droplets hitting the floor.

"That's when it became real," confided Brenda. "With the sound of the dripping, I realized how brutal it was. It just hit me how tragic it was."

Though Brenda had planned just one visit to the murder site, she and the team found themselves heading back several more times. "The house kept drawing us back," said Brenda. "We kept thinking we were finished with the investigation, and then we would find ourselves back there again."

The psychics zeroed in on two men as the culprits. One, they believe, was a hired killer, and the other was his accomplice. The accomplice was unaware that the children would become victims and has great remorse over the fact. He is, they say, so sorry that he has returned to the Villisca home.

As for the children, Catherine suffered the most. "We believe that she woke up during the attack," said Brenda. The little girl, the psychics felt, hid in a closet but was yanked out and slaughtered on her bed. The investigators got an audio tape recording of a young girl's voice saying, "I'm dying."

The Third Eye   **59**

It is a devastating scenario, one that seems to have no hope. Yet, amidst the cruelty and violence, a single powerful message shines through. "It is why we were there," said Brenda, who feels that the spirits of the tragedy called upon them so they might speak on their behalf.

"The Moores were a very spiritual family," explained Brenda.

Sarah, in particular, took the teachings of her church to heart. The loving mother and devout Christian carried her values with her to her death. From the other side, she spoke one word so loudly and clearly that the Miller Paranormal team was able to capture it on audio tape.

"Forgiveness."

THE VILLISCA AXE MURDER HOUSE AND OLSON-LINN MUSEUM
323 East Fourth Street
Villisca, IA 50864
(712) 621-4291

Buyer Beware

In the early 1990s, while I was writing regularly for *Woman's World* magazine, my editors assigned me a story about psychics who work with detectives to solve crimes.

I talked extensively with Dorothy Allison, a Nutley, New Jersey, psychic, and featured her in the article. Since her death in 1999 at age 74, Dorothy has alternately been called the most famous psychic in the twentieth century and a fraud.

Critics gather data about all the times that Dorothy was wrong. I doubt there has ever been a psychic who was 100 percent correct.

Psychics are simply people, as flawed as all other human beings, who happen to have minds that tune into information to which the rest of the population may not be privy. Some of it comes through clearly, while some of it is disjointed and pointless.

Dorothy Allison's landmark case was in 1967. She awoke from a horrible dream with a pounding headache. In her nightmare, she had seen a little boy. His shoes were on the wrong feet, and a note was pinned to his shirt. The child was stuck in a pipe.

Unable to shake the vision, she went to the police with the information. She had never met five-year-old Michael Kurcsics and had no way of knowing that the motherless boy's shoes were indeed on the wrong feet.

Temperatures had been freezing in New Jersey, but when it warmed up, the pipe where the drowned child had been stuck thawed, and he popped out. He was just as Dorothy had described, right down to the note (for his teacher) that had been pinned to his shirt.

After Dorothy's dream, the ordinary housewife soon became a well-known psychic.

When I spoke with her, she was exhausted. "The mothers keep calling me," she told me, explaining how it tore at her heart to hear from so many desperate mothers with missing children.

After three decades of working with detectives, she did not want to work on murder cases any longer. Yet, she could not turn away cases that involved children. She vowed to continue helping the little ones but had no energy left to work on cases that involved adults. She had to draw the line somewhere.

I felt sorry for her. She sounded so unhappy and so tired. But, as she pointed out, if she turned her back, killers would walk free, and more children would be hurt.

I suspect that one of the reasons that Dorothy has been so criticized is that though she was extremely psychic, she was basically an ordinary woman of average intelligence who was not particularly media savvy. She was passionate about helping to solve crimes, but because she was rough around the edges, she sometimes offended people.

As directed by my *Woman's World* editors, I interviewed a detective who had worked with Dorothy, and he was pleased to offer his praise.

He told me of the time that the psychic had dropped by the office to chat. Though they had not publicized a homicide case they were working on, Dorothy suddenly said, "Tell me about the black woman on the railroad tracks."

They had not mentioned the case to her, he said, and Dorothy had no way of knowing about it—except through her sixth sense.

"She told us that the killer had a metal plate in his head. She also said that he would be arrested for an unrelated crime and kill himself in jail, and that he would be wearing army boots."

Everything Dorothy told them came to be.

For my readers who may be seeking advice from a psychic, remember that few will have the abilities that Dorothy Allison had. And remember, that she, too, was limited.

The fact that a psychic is featured regularly on television does not necessarily mean that they are particularly gifted. One famous psychic, who will remain unnamed, charges hundreds per hour and has so many fans that they have to wait over a year to give her their hard-earned cash. Yet, her predictions have rarely been validated.

Buyer Beware!

𝕲𝖍𝖔𝖘𝖙𝖘 𝖎𝖓 𝖙𝖍𝖊 𝕹𝖊𝖜𝖘

Clearly Heard

A TEARFUL MOTHER testified in a German court that a pair of psychics led her to her daughter's killer, according to a January 4, 2005, edition of the *Expatica Direct Newsletter,* which translates German to English.

Sigrid Erbe, forty-five, told the court of her heartbreak when her sixteen-year-old daughter was murdered in June 2003. Frustrated when the killer eluded detectives, she contacted the mediums. The spirit of Susanne was apparently lingering on the other side, because she came through to the psychics and fingered her murderer.

The psychics "told me he was a Croatian man in his mid-twenties, and they told me where to look for him at a garage in Mannheim," testified the grieving mother.

When she passed the information along to the investigators, they took it to heart and tracked down twenty-four-year-old Mario Glavic. Just as the dead girl had told the psychics, he was a Croat and employed at a Mannheim garage. Mario Glavic confessed to the murder, saying that he was drunk and on cocaine, and though he had attacked her, he had not meant for her to die. He had struck the girl with a rock in an effort to quiet her when she began to scream.

He may have silenced her for awhile, but in the end, Susanne's voice was clearly heard.

four

Witch Hunt

*I do testify that I have seen Margaret Rule in her afflictions from
the invisible world, lifted up from her bed, wholly by an invisible force,
a great way towards the top of the room where she lay; in her being so
lifted, she had no assistance from any use of her own arms or hands,
or any other part of her body, not so much as her heels touching her
bed, or resting on any support whatsoever . . .*

Witness my hand,
Samuel Aves

Samuel Aves was one of several men who signed sworn testimonies
stating that they had witnessed Margaret Rule levitate. The accusation
came in the wake of the 1692 Salem witch trials.

Though few people think of Boston, Massachusetts, when it comes
to the infamous witch episode, it, too, suffered from the irrational wor-
ries that the Puritans forced upon Salem.

Margaret Rule was seventeen in 1693 when she was accused of
being a witch in Boston.

I have a special interest in her dramatic saga, because a drop of her
blood runs through my veins.

We are family.

Born nearly three centuries apart, we, of course, have never met.
Yet we are bonded by a thin thread of genetics that spans time.

My first view of Boston was from a 747, my forehead pressed against the cool glass of the window, an airsickness bag clutched in my hand.

A plane full of people had just heard me be sick, and I didn't care. With a horrible headache and a stomach that threatened to rebel again, I felt too ill to care what anyone thought.

Was it a bad sandwich from the Sea-Tac Airport, or was this an emotional response to the horrors that the city below had once inflicted upon so many people?

I had wanted to visit Boston all of my life, but now the view from the sky made my head hurt more.

The city looked brown and barren. I could not stop thinking of how frightening it must have been to be marched to the gallows. Were the accused witches sick to their stomachs, as I was now?

By the next day, my stomach had settled, and I began to appreciate the historic views that Boston offered.

I had chosen a hotel one block from the Boston Common, the haunted park where accused witches were hanged, and where ghosts are seen by visitors.

Since 1634, the people of Boston have claimed the Common as their own. The once scrubby land of rolling hills served as a place for citizens to graze their cattle. Families were limited to one cow or four sheep apiece.

The site, however, was not merely a peaceful, pastoral scene. It was a place of dark deeds—deeds sanctioned by law, but so horrible that the victims still cry for justice.

Though the Boston Common retains the basic configuration of its early days, Puritans would probably not recognize it. A spider web of paved paths cuts through the forty-plus acres. Features include a band-stand, a baseball field, and the Frog Pond, a small lake that sparkles in the sunshine.

The Boston Common may be the most haunted site in town. (Leslie Rule)

Countless couples fall in love on the Common, babies giggle with delight as they toss nuts to the squirrels, and families picnic here. Despite the happy times, tragedy still marks the environment.

Before my Margaret, there was Margaret Jones. A midwife from nearby Charlestown, she was convicted of casting a spell to kill her

As night creeps close, the trees cast long shadows upon the Common. (Leslie Rule)

neighbor's cow. On June 5, 1648, Margaret Jones was hanged on the Boston Common.

A magnificent elm tree was used for the many hangings of those of whom the Puritans did not approve. They also hung pirates and Quakers from the old tree.

When caretakers lock the gate of the Common's Central Burial Ground, they keep the living out but cannot keep the dead in. (Leslie Rule)

On October 27, 1659, authorities hanged Quakers Marmaduke Stevenson and William Robinson on the Common. Quaker Mary Dyer was next in line. As she stood with a noose around her neck, and the bodies of the others dangling before her, her son convinced the men to release her. They escorted her from the city and told her to stay away. Less than a year later, Mary returned. She was hanged on the Common on June 1, 1660.

Margaret Rule's troubles began about three years later, on September 10, 1663.

She and her parents, from Cornwall, England, had come by ship to the new land and lived in north Boston. Her parents had a reputation as "sober and honest." But Margaret was judged by her own actions when she "fell into odd fits" in public. Her friends carried her home, and nosy neighbors came by to peer at her.

Some suspected that Margaret's affliction was caused by a "miserable woman," who was once jailed for witchcraft. This woman claimed that she could cure people by chanting over them and the very night before had threatened Margaret.

This view from the Boston Common shows the Little Building (at left). Do those murdered on the Common visit the Little Building? (Leslie Rule)

When their family members were buried here two centuries ago, mourners could never have imagined the enormous buildings that today look down upon the Common and its graveyard. (Leslie Rule)

Investigators believed that Margaret was being "assaulted by eight cruel specters." It was alleged that the "cursed specters" demanded that she put her hand on a thick, red book and vow to become a servant of the devil.

How in the world did anyone come to that conclusion?

Did Margaret say she saw eight specters?

What was wrong with the teenager?

Perhaps she had epilepsy. Perhaps she had an overactive imagination. Whatever the reason, Margaret was in serious trouble.

As I wandered through the Common, I wondered if Margaret had also walked the grounds. What did she think when she saw the enormous elm with its thick, reaching branches?

Had she been present for any of the executions? Did she have any idea that she could soon be swinging from the death tree, a rope around her frail, white neck?

I was about Margaret's age when I found myself in a similar predicament. Though there was never any danger of hanging or incarceration, I, too, became known as a witch.

Trees grow near the spot where the magnificent death tree once reined. These trees carry the genes of the famous elm, just as I carry the genes of accused witch Margaret Rule, who narrowly escaped hanging from the elm's cruel branches. (Leslie Rule)

I was attending Mount Rainier High School in Des Moines, Washington, when I made a silly, flip comment about my nail polish. Another girl commented on the glitter-embedded polish, and I jokingly said, "Oh, I'm a witch. They turn this way every year around Halloween."

Within two weeks, I could not walk down the hallway at school without someone putting a mock spell on me or shouting, "Witch!" To this day, there are people in my hometown who still believe the rumors that exploded from the stupid joke I made about my nails.

The experience gave me just a little taste of how fast a rumor can grow. Is that what happened to Margaret Rule?

According to archives, Margaret fasted for nine days. Yet she remained "fresh" and "lively" and "hearty." When food was forced upon her, she gritted her teeth.

In addition to swearing that they had seen Margaret levitate, people said they had witnessed unseen hands force her mouth open and pour "something invisible" down her throat. Some alleged that they saw the substance spill on her neck. Margaret screamed as if "scalding brimstone" had been poured on her.

It was also said that Margaret looked sad, as she claimed that ghosts threatened to drown a young man in the neighborhood. It was later

A plaque marks the ground where the elm grew until 1876. (Leslie Rule)

determined that at the exact time she made the prediction, a man had nearly drowned.

Cotton Mather, one of those who examined Margaret, noted that the specters surrounding her were identical to those seen surrounding the accused witches in Salem, months before. It has been written that if it had been up to Cotton Mather, Margaret and others would have been executed.

Centuries of weather have washed away the names of those buried here in the Central Burial Ground. (Leslie Rule)

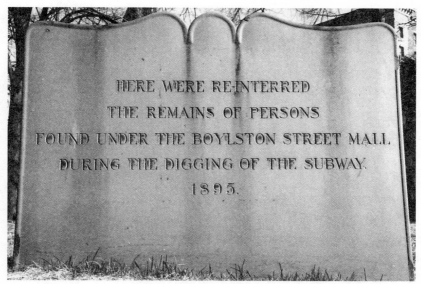

HERE WERE RE-INTERRED
THE REMAINS OF PERSONS
FOUND UNDER THE BOYLSTON STREET MALL
DURING THE DIGGING OF THE SUBWAY.
1895.

Are the displaced dead displeased with their mass burial in the Central Burial Ground? (Leslie Rule)

But Robert Calef, a prominent Boston merchant, also studied Margaret. He stated that she was either faking or under a delusion. After a few trying weeks, Margaret began to feel normal again.

She and her parents returned to Cornwall, where my great-grandfather was born a few generations later.

If Robert Calef had not made his levelheaded assessment, Margaret Rule could have been one of the ghosts who wander the Boston Common.

The ethereal image of a woman has been seen in the old graveyard there. The cemetery is on the edge of the Common, bordering Boylston Street. Many of the stones here are so old that the lettering has worn away.

Holly Mascott Nadler, author of *Ghosts of Boston Town: Three Centuries of True Hauntings,* reported a ghost sighting in the Common cemetery. On a drizzly afternoon in the 1970s, a dentist named Dr. Matt Rutger decided to wander in the tranquil beauty of the ancient graveyard and encountered "a total deviation from reality as most of us know it," she wrote.

As the dentist attempted to read the worn lettering on the weather-washed gravestones, he was startled by a tap on his shoulder. When he swung around to see who had touched him, no one was there. According to Holly, the incident repeated itself until it escalated to a violent tug on the back of his coat collar that nearly knocked him down. The frightened dentist had turned to leave when, he said, "I saw a young girl standing motionless in the rear of the cemetery, staring at me intently."

The girl in the white dress was eerily still. When the dentist turned to the opposite direction, the ghost "relocated."

Holly Mascott Nadler wrote that the apparition continued to appear each time the dentist changed his path. When he reached the sidewalk, he felt a hand slip into his pocket and watched, stunned, as his keys levitated and then dropped to the ground.

I was fascinated by Holly's account and wondered if the ghost belonged to one of those buried in the old cemetery on the Common.

Or was she the unhappy spirit of someone long-ago lynched?

Do the ghosts of executed Quakers, pirates, and accused witches wander the Common? (Leslie Rule)

A ghostly woman has been spotted on the Boston Common. (Leslie Rule)

While the formal graveyard is neatly lined by a tall metal fence, it is not the only place where bodies are buried in the Boston Common.

In the old days, authorities liked to make an example of the executed and would often leave them in public view, long after death.

Buildings along Boylston Street rest on top of the old graveyard. The tenants of the desecrated graves may be responsible for the odd noises that emanate from the basement of the cigar shop. (Leslie Rule)

The insult was too much for the relatives of the dead to stand. Some of them tiptoed into the Common in the midst of night and hastily buried their loved ones in unmarked graves.

I explored the Common in the light of day, stopping passersby to inquire if they had ever witnessed a ghost there. I admittedly got my share of odd looks.

Every other person had a cell phone pressed to an ear. I should not have been surprised that they had not noticed the dead when they barely noticed the living!

I ventured into the shops on the streets that lined the Common to continue my inquiries. In an art store on Tremont Street, I learned that an employee had witnessed a shadowy figure darting through the basement. Bouncers at a nightclub on the same street are spooked by the shenanigans of an unseen presence. Sometimes after the club has closed and the doors are locked, the sound system will come back on, the volume turned to full blast.

Boylston Street, too, has paranormal activity. The old cemetery once extended to the space that the street now occupies. A huge section of the graveyard was lopped off to make room for the street. As shovels churned up the earth, the skeletons that surfaced were plucked out and buried in a common grave. The rest of the dead reside below Boylston Street and its buildings, sleeping restlessly in their desecrated graves.

Some students of Emerson College who live in Boylston Street's Little Building, a stone's toss from the graveyard, believe their residence is haunted. In addition to sensing a presence there, they have noted that the elevator has a mind of its own. It sometimes stops on the floors of its choice, as if picking up invisible passengers.

While they have attributed this to the legend of a little girl who took a fatal tumble down the elevator shaft, the ghosts of the Common could also be responsible.

Stephen Smith, of L. J. Peretti Co. Tobacconists has heard the inexplicable rattle of chains in the early morning hours when he is alone in the building. The metallic clanks emanate from the empty basement, where there is no reasonable explanation for the sound.

Though he can't say for certain that the noise is of a paranormal nature, he admitted the incidents are chilling.

Chains?

Some quick research revealed that accused witches and other prisoners in seventeenth-century New England were indeed bound with chains.

Of all the places I investigated near the Boston Common, the most haunted has room for many ghosts and a two-hundred-year-old proprietor who makes sure that everyone is comfortable.

Do any of the ghosts who reside at the Omni Parker House hotel originate from the fatal limbs of the old elm?

Read on and make your own decision.

A **Ghost** for a Host

James Smith stepped into the room across from the ballroom and froze. A shadowy figure had just rushed past him. He whirled around, trying to get a closer look, but the thing had vanished as quickly as it had appeared. He shuddered and went back to work.

After working many years as a bartender at the Omni Parker House hotel, he takes the unusual happenings in stride. "We have employees who are too afraid to go to the ballroom alone," he told me, as he escorted me to the large room with the rounded ceiling.

James is not afraid, but he normally does not talk about the ghosts. We took the crowded service elevator as he gave me a quick tour of the most haunted spots in the hotel. The male employees who shared the elevator appeared spooked when I asked them if they had ever encountered ghosts in the hotel. They all shook their heads no, but something in their eyes told me they were fibbing.

The Omni Parker House, a short walk from the Common, is crawling with ghosts. (Leslie Rule)

James Smith is one of the few Omni Parker House employees brave enough to go to the ballroom alone. (Leslie Rule)

"People say they've seen ghosts on the sixth floor," James told me. It is usually a fleeting glimpse, but full-figured apparitions have been spotted there.

Years ago an elderly woman saw a ghost outside of room 1078. It materialized as an indefinable cloud and gradually took the shape of a man. The heavy-set gentleman with the black moustache stared at her for a moment and then vanished.

Everyone said that she had seen the ghost of Harvey Parker.

He was a twenty-year-old farm boy with barely a dollar to his name when he arrived in Boston in 1825. Seven years later he was a restaurant owner, but his ambitions did not end there. In 1855 he opened the grandest hotel the city had ever seen.

Harvey died at seventy-nine in 1884. Many believe the perfectionist still tries to run the hotel and often helps out.

But why would he throw teapots? Waitress Heather Alvarado was startled when she was in a storage room, and the pots seemed to leap off the shelf toward her.

Maybe Harvey is not alone. Maybe he is surrounded by a few less helpful ghosts. The area has seen more than its share of violent death, partly due to its proximity to the Boston Common.

Do those who were so cruelly executed there creep over to the hotel?

If they do, Harvey would surely make them feel welcome. He had a reputation for playing the consummate host to the wealthiest guests or the most ordinary of citizens.

A. Hafeez Yassin agrees that Harvey is among the ghosts who wander the hotel. He was alone in the ballroom one day, cleaning up after a party and listening to reggae music on his radio. Suddenly, the station abruptly changed, skimming over a dozen channels until it settled on a classical station. "That's the kind of music that Harvey would have listened to," he said.

Another employee was exhausted after a long day but had not quite finished his work in the ballroom. He had one more table to set up. He left the room for a moment, and when he returned, the table had been magically set. He looked around astonished. No one else had been in the area.

It was probably Harvey, he figured, still helping out at the hotel that had made him a multimillionaire.

OMNI PARKER HOUSE
60 School Street
Boston, MA 02108
(617) 227-8600

Ghosts of Salem

When most folks think of Salem, Massachusetts, they conjure images of witches in tall, crooked hats, riding brooms against a full moon. It is an image that the city has done little to discourage.

It was 1692 when teenaged girls began acting silly and sparked a hysteria that burned through Salem Village. The little town (now known as Danvers) was near today's city of Salem.

The teenagers' odd behavior was blamed on the devil, and soon neighbor was accusing neighbor of witchcraft. Many residents were jailed as accused witches, including a four-year-old girl.

In the horrific end, nineteen people were hanged and one was crushed to death.

The murder of twenty innocent people may very well account for the paranormal activity that swirls around the area today, including some of the following places:

First to Die

According to the managers of the Lyceum Restaurant, the classy eatery was built atop Bridget Bishop's old apple orchard. The very first villager hanged for witchcraft, Bridget was a colorful character who managed to annoy her neighbors with her flamboyant dress and her tendency to speak her mind.

It is Bridget's spirit who is responsible for the odd noises heard at the Lyceum, say employees.

When my friends Anne and Hilary Ferraro and I visited the restaurant, the manager invited us to explore the unoccupied upper floors. We were tired after walking around town all day, so after we had ventured up to the second floor, Anne turned to her daughter, twenty-

Some employees refuse to venture upstairs in the Lyceum Bar and Grill. This view is from the loft, where strange noises often emanate. (Leslie Rule)

one-year-old Hilary, and said, "Go up to the loft and tell us if there is anything worth seeing."

Hilary obediently started up the stairs. She was three-quarters of the way up when an ominous creak sounded from above, and suddenly Hilary was flying back down the stairs.

We all headed up to investigate. What could have caused the creak? It was so loud that we had all heard it. It had sounded like the creaking door in a scary movie. I tried all of the loft doors but could not duplicate the sound.

According to the manager, a film crew had visited recently to document the haunting and was baffled when the batteries were inexplicably deleted on every piece of their recording equipment, a common occurrence in haunted locations.

LYCEUM BAR AND GRILL

43 Church Street

Salem, MA 01970

(978) 745-7665

Web site: www.LyceumSalem.com

Ghostly Witch

A formidable brick house, erected in 1784, may be home to the ghost of Sheriff George Corwin. The Joshua Ward House, which today houses offices, was built on the foundation of the home of one of Salem's most detested people.

George Corwin was a cruel man who orchestrated the arrest of villagers accused of witchcraft. Many hated him after he tortured the accused in his home. He also stole the victims' belongings after they were executed on Gallows Hill.

When George Corwin died, he was buried in his own basement to prevent his enemies from desecrating his grave. He was later exhumed and buried elsewhere, but many believe the despicable man's spirit remains.

Who peers from the windows of the Joshua Ward House? (Leslie Rule)

It is a woman's ghost, however, that has been spotted in the house. One witness saw the pale woman sitting in a chair in the home, while others have spied her peeking from the windows, or floating down the stairs. It is said that she is one of the accused witches who died as a result of Sheriff Corwin's actions.

JOSHUA WARD HOUSE
148 Washington Street
Salem, MA 01970
(The Joshua Ward House is not open to the public.)

Derby Street Haunting

Some believe it is the proximity to the city's oldest graveyard that stirs up the ghosts in Roosevelt's Restaurant. Owner Henry McGowan told a reporter for the North Andover, Massachusetts, *Eagle-Tribune* in October 2001, that he realized the place was haunted when items began moving around on their own.

An artist sculpted ghostly figures emerging from the wall outside of Roosevelt's Restaurant. The wall supports one end of the old graveyard. (Leslie Rule)

The owner of Roosevelt's Restaurant in Salem met the ghost of a woman here. (Leslie Rule)

He spotted an apparition when he was working alone in the building until three a.m. "I was on the second floor," he said. "I actually looked up and saw somebody looking down at me. It was a woman." He looked away for an instant, and when he looked back, she had vanished.

The building's outdoor courtyard showcases a bit of whimsical and eerie art. A stone wall stops the graveyard next door from tumbling onto his property. Henry hired an artist to sculpt the images of ghosts, climbing through the wall, as if they were escaping from the cemetery.

According to legend, a casket once broke through the wall and fell into the building. Employees insist it really happened and point to part of the wall that obviously has been patched.

No one knows the identity of the ghosts who wander through the restaurant, but some wonder if they may indeed have escaped from the cemetery next door.

Known as the Burying Point, the graveyard is the final resting place of a judge from the Salem Witch Trials.

ROOSEVELT'S RESTAURANT
300 Derby Street
Salem, MA 01970
(978) 745-1133

Gallows Hill

Mollie Stewart, a well-known paranormal researcher who leads the Vampire and Ghost Tour and owns the Spellbound Museum, was conducting an investigation on Gallows Hill one night when she encountered a presence.

Gallows Hill, a few miles from Salem, is infamous as the spot where nineteen accused witches were hanged.

As Mollie ventured up the hill, she at first didn't think too much of it when she heard voices. She figured it was just a few other people, out exploring. But then she spotted a hooded figure. As she stared, it vanished before her eyes.

The voices grew quiet, and she found no sign that other living beings had been there that night.

SPELLBOUND MUSEUM

190 Essex Street

Salem, MA 01947

(978) 745-0138

Web site: www.spellboundtours.com

Evil Avoided

While hunting for ghosts, I not only found my roots but discovered an enemy.

If Cotton Mather had had his way, I would not be here today. Not only did the self-righteous Puritan oppose Margaret Rule, from my

William Penn first landed in Old New Castle, Delaware, near the site of this dock. When I stood on this dock, I had a profound sense of connection with the area but did not yet know that my great-great-great-great-great-great-grandfather Thomas Stackhouse had been here with William Penn. Not only did Cotton Mather want to execute my relative, Margaret Rule, but he also wished to sell William Penn and my ancestor into slavery. (Leslie Rule)

father's side of the family, he proposed selling my ancestors on my mother's side into slavery.

My great-great-great-great-great-great-grandfather, Thomas Stackhouse, traveled here via ship with William Penn in 1682. When Cotton Mather heard that twenty-three ships carrying Quakers were on their way from England, he proposed kidnapping the passengers and selling them into slavery. His bright idea came a decade before he stirred up the Massachusetts witch controversy.

But destiny had its own plan. Both the Stackhouse and the Rule lines survived, and here I am, seven generations later, researching the ghosts of those who died at the hands of Cotton Mather.

"I wonder how many people he killed?" said my mother, Ann Stackhouse Rule, as she pondered the evil deeds of the Boston minister.

I have walked the paths that Mr. Mather walked, and have spoken to those who have encountered the ghosts of his victims. I've stood on the dock in Old New Castle, Delaware, where William Penn and my ancestor arrived on October 27, 1682.

It is here, on the Delaware River, where headless apparitions have been witnessed. I did not see the ghosts, believed to be Dutch soldiers, but could almost hear the sound of their whispering beneath the rush of the waves.

History's harsh lessons and the ghosts they have wrought make me acutely aware of the fragility of life. From the murder of accused witch Bridget Bishop in Salem to Quaker Mary Dyer hanged on the Boston Common, the deaths were cruel and ugly.

While the unjust killings silenced the heartbeat, they did not stop the spirit.

Survivors carry family names. Ghosts still wander their old homesteads. And, despite Cotton Mather's objections, William Penn founded Pennsylvania.

Cotton Mather is buried in Boston's Copps Hill Burying Ground. I won't be putting flowers on his grave.

five

The Enemy Within

When I stayed at the Heathman Hotel in Portland, Oregon, in 2001, I did not ask for a haunted room. In fact, I did not yet know the hotel was haunted.

I had checked in to meet with Diana Jordan, who has a syndicated radio program called *Between the Lines*.

My first ghost book, *Coast to Coast Ghosts: True Stories of Hauntings Across America*, had just come out, and she had scheduled an interview.

My room was 702. I thought it odd when the bedside lamp turned itself off and on but figured it was just a short in the wiring.

Diana taped the interview in my room and picked up a background static that was so bad that she almost couldn't air it.

"I decided to use it and play up the fact that the disturbance might be from the hotel's ghost," she told me.

We had learned that it was common knowledge among the hotel staff that all of the rooms ending with two were haunted.

I soon discovered why when I searched Portland's newspaper archives. In December 1965, a man who had worked long years at a nearby restaurant had been promised a promotion when new management took over the business. Instead, he was fired.

Devastated, he went to the top of the Heathman and jumped to his death.

My guess is that his fall took him past the row of windows that belonged to the rooms ending in two.

One of the saddest things about suicide is the fact that depressed folks don't have to suffer or die.

Not anymore.

Chemists have figured out how to balance the human brain so that many who are depressed can feel calm and hopeful again. All types of drugs are now available, and with a little patience and persistence, those who suffer from mental anguish often can find the medication to set their brain chemistry right.

Depression is not a weakness. It is a physical imbalance in the brain that affects millions of people. The medicine helps makes the depressed person's brain function as it is supposed to.

When they are in the grips of depression, however, people cannot believe that they will ever feel better. Some take drastic measures, and sadly, find themselves forever trapped in the gloom.

The following are examples of people with no hope, who are now truly stuck in a hopeless place.

In Uniform

The theatergoers at the Guthrie Theater in Minneapolis, Minnesota, had had enough.

How could they enjoy the movie when the usher kept walking in front of them?

Finally, one woman got up from her seat and went out to the lobby. There, she found the head usher and complained about the disruptive usher. He listened as she described the teenager who kept blocking her view. A chill went through him.

Her description certainly matched one of their employees. But he no longer worked at the theater. He was dead, buried in his usher's uniform, weeks before. The eighteen-year-old had shot himself in the head.

It was early spring 1967, and the ghost sightings were both frightening and sad. Some of the boy's coworkers wished they had been kinder to him. They hadn't realized how lonely he was.

The kid with the English accent had seemed out of place with others his age. Gawky and shy, he did not make friends easily. Few went out of their way to include him.

According to Minneapolis residents, the ghost of the lonely boy was seen long after his death, usually patrolling row 18. It had been one of his regularly assigned areas.

Eventually, the theater was "cleansed," and no sightings of the ghostly usher have been reported since.

GUTHRIE THEATER
725 Vineland Place
Minneapolis, MN 55403
(612) 377-2224

Still Pining

The Carneal House Inn in Covington, Kentucky, is home to the melancholy spirit of a woman scorned. Constructed in 1820 in the center of the city's historic Riverside district, the huge, antebellum-style house was originally named Southgate House.

Legend has it that Marquis de Lafayette attended a party there and was unresponsive to the batting eyes of a young lady who fell for him. Rejected and distraught, she took her own life in an upstairs bedroom.

Visitors to the bed and breakfast have glimpsed the spirit of a woman in a gray silk dress. She has been witnessed floating down the carved wooden staircase and seen pacing on the second-story balcony. When the rocking chair rocks on its own, many believe her ghost is present.

THE CARNEAL HOUSE INN

405 E. Second Street

Covington, KY 41011

(606) 431-6130

Troubled Waters

The remnants of a century-old railroad bridge straddle White Lick Creek in Danville, Indiana. The mournful howling heard here is believed by many to be the disturbed spirit of a young woman who met her fate on a bleak night.

According to one version of the legend, she was a young mother with a babe in arms whose family had turned her away. In her day, unwed mothers were shunned. The girl did not know where to turn. She found herself alone and began to wander along the railroad track. As she stumbled over the bridge, she hugged her baby close, wondering how in the world she would support the infant.

Her choices grew even grimmer when she heard the train barreling toward her. There was no time to run. She could stay and be plowed down by the train, or jump off of the bridge to almost certain death. She leapt from the bridge, but it was not the end, for her confused spirit still clings to the concrete structure.

Yet another story says that the ghostly screams belong to a worker who fell into the wet cement during construction of the bridge. His body has been entombed there ever since.

Skeptics say the sound of the screams is nothing more than the wind whistling through the arches of the bridge, but others insist it is the cries of a frightened woman.

Vestiges of the Danville Interurban Bridge are located at the north end of Ellis Park.

Bridge to Death

Earthbound spirits roam the Washington Avenue Bridge in Minneapolis, according to students of the University of Minnesota. Four traffic lanes wide with an enclosed heated walkway, the double-decker bridge spans the Mississippi River. It connects the east and west banks of the Minneapolis campus, and, for some, life to death.

Sadly, this bridge is the site where so many depressed people have jumped to their doom that it has been deemed "one of the most popular suicide spots in the city."

On a Friday morning in 1972, acclaimed poet and University of Minnesota professor John Berryman climbed over the railing of the bridge and leapt into the cold, calculating arms of the Grim Reaper.

The Pulitzer Prize–winning poet had wrestled with alcoholism for the previous six months, and in the end, a bottle of whiskey won the match. Not quite sixty years old, the sensitive soul whose words had moved so many simply could not take the pain of his life any longer. The irony is that, now, he may be trapped in that agony.

Some who linger on the bridge say they have heard the sound of footsteps moving toward them when no living person is in sight. The phantom pacing is attributed to the dead poet and others who died there.

The University of Minnesota's Twin Cities Campus is east of downtown Minneapolis.

(612) 625-5000

Fatal Step

It took seven million man-hours to construct the most famous building in our country. And it takes 1,860 stair steps to reach the top. Yet, it takes just one step to end a life.

Since the completion of New York's Empire State Building in 1931, nearly three dozen troubled people have taken a fatal step off the building.

In one irreversible step into empty sky, they believed they were saying good-bye to their pain. Unfortunately, nothing is that easy, for the ghosts of suicide victims have long been seen in the 102-story building.

If they had only let time take care of their woes, their hurt may have eventually vanished. But because they could not bear to wait it out, they are stuck in their torment indefinitely.

Photographers have gotten fascinating anomalies in shots taken from the top of the building, including spirit-like streaks that appear to be exiting the structure. Among the wraiths that are said to be wandering the Empire State Building is that of a broken-hearted young woman in 1940s fashion.

THE EMPIRE STATE BUILDING IS IN MIDTOWN MANHATTAN
BETWEEN 33RD AND 34TH STREETS AT:
350 Fifth Avenue
New York, NY 10118
(877) 692-8439
www.esbnyc.com

EMPIRE STATE BUILDING
NEW YORK

IRVING
UNDERHILL

This 1930s postcard depicts the Empire State Building, where many suicide victims are stuck indefinitely. (author's collection)

Ghosts in the News

Closing Time

SUICIDE DID NOT END the sad saga of a woman on North Dixie Drive in Dayton, Ohio, according to the October 28, 1999, issue of the *Dayton Daily News*. The specter, known as the "lady in red," appeared in the Odd Lots store on North Dixie Drive and liked to handle the merchandise.

Employee Lorna Boggs told reporter Martha Hardcastle that toys sometimes flew off of shelves when no living person was near them.

Store employees believed the ghost may be that of a woman who allegedly hung herself in the warehouse portion of the building when it was operated as Liberal Market.

One evening after hours, Lorna Boggs was doing her paperwork when she saw a woman lingering in the store. She was about to open her mouth to announce that the store was closed when she stopped herself.

It was not a shopper; it was a ghost.

"She had a red dress hanging out from a black coat, and she was wearing black shoes and a black straw hat," Lorna told the reporter.

The "lady in red" may not be aware she has already checked out.

six

Victims of War

When it comes to killing, there is one instance where many consider it to be a noble deed.

War.

Millions of people have killed each other for things such as honor and land and have been heralded as heroes. Indeed, these folks may very well be selfless and brave with nothing but the best intentions in their hearts. But that fact does not diminish the ugliness of violent death or the grief of those who lose loved ones in battle.

War has probably produced more earthbound spirits than any other type of death. The sheer number of war victims and the fact that most dead soldiers were cut down in the prime of their lives result in a mind-boggling number of stuck souls. Here are a few cases of mortally wounded warriors who remain.

Reporting for Duty

One location that may harbor the ghosts of war victims is a forty-five-minute ferry ride from Seattle. The naval shipyard in Bremerton, Washington, is a place where old submarines go to die. The following are excerpts of a correspondence from a witness to strange goings on there.

Hello Leslie,

I guess that one would classify me as a "sensitive guy," in that I always felt a deep closeness to religious and spiritual matters and could somehow feel things about certain people, houses, and situations.

Two of my experiences that involve the paranormal occurred while I was employed with the Puget Sound Naval Shipyard in Bremerton, Washington. Both occurred in Dry-dock #3, aboard nuclear submarines that were undergoing inactivation and recycling.

The first happened on the SSN-665 Guitarro *on 8/16/94. I worked blowing down the engine room section of the submarine, following abrasive blast operations to remove surface contaminants. The metal had to be cleaned prior to being cut and sold for scrap.*

On this warm August day, there were only two people in the area. No sooner had I started blowing down with the blast hose when I heard my name called. . . .

So began the letter from Roger Maggert, who went on to explain that though the equipment produced noise louder than a jet engine, the voice was clear. He climbed off the submarine and asked his puzzled coworker if he had called to him.

Roger went back to work but heard his name called several more times. Sure that someone was playing a trick on him, he checked to see if someone was hiding atop the submarine. When he found no one there, he returned to work, shaken. *As I continued with the blow-down,* he wrote, *I became aware of fifteen to twenty voices all talking at once. It was as if a party were happening inside that sub. . . .*

The voices escalated until Roger became so rattled that he finally grabbed his gear and left. His second encounter was four years later on October 10, 1998. Again, he was working with just one other man in the recycling area of the Bremerton shipyard, this time on the *SSN-660 Sand Lance.* Roger wrote:

I caught movement from the corner of my eye through my MSA full-face respirator. I turned to witness a full-figure ghost staring directly at me for at least fifteen seconds! This man was about ten feet from me, wore dark blue navy coveralls and was about five feet ten inches. He was balding and held what appeared to be a flashlight. He seemed to be in his late forties, and was possibly of Slavic descent. Without saying a word, he implanted the following statements in my mind. "Why are you doing away with my home?" and, "It's not polite to stare."

It was clear that this man did not know he was dead. . . .

Roger obligingly glanced at the ground, and when he looked back, the ghost had vanished before his eyes. His letter continues: *I marveled that I had truly seen a ghost. In fact, I was so excited that I called a trusted friend who worked with me and confided that something weird had happened. . . .*

Before he could explain, his friend told him that he had seen an apparition when he was sandblasting the night before Roger's encounter. The two men were incredulous. The shared encounter created a special tie between them, said Roger.

When he asked around, he learned that a chief had died of a heart attack on the *Sand Lance*. He could not find documentation of the death but suspects the ghost he encountered was the chief.

It is also possible that the specter who stalks the Bremerton shipyard is tied to one of the many deaths connected with the site. Perhaps he was one of the crew of the USS *Saratoga*, an aircraft carrier launched in 1925. Its wartime résumé included carrying planes that brought death and destruction to the Japanese.

The ship was attacked on February 21, 1945, near Iwo Jima. Six Japanese planes scored five hits within a three-minute span. The surviving crew, though stunned by the sight of their dead shipmates, scrambled to extinguish the fires raging on the hangar deck. They were heartbroken to find that 123 of their own were killed or missing.

Less than four weeks later, the *Saratoga* arrived at the Bremerton shipyard for repairs.

Could it have brought a few ghosts along? Perhaps the dead men followed their shipmates off of the *Saratoga* and took refuge in the shipyard.

Could a few of them have found their way into the old submarine that Roger prepared for recycling? Maybe. Most likely the noisy party that Roger heard was a place memory, imprinted upon the submarine by the men who had once lived there.

When it comes to speculating on the identities of those who haunt the shipyard, we have many from which to choose. In addition to those killed in battle, there are other deaths connected with the place.

The Bremerton shipyard is notorious as the site that launched the 1918 pandemic in the state of Washington, the fatal flu that wiped out 20 percent of America's population. With one out of five folks succumbing, nearly every family lost someone.

According to William Dietrich's article, "The Enemy Within," in the October 24, 2004, issue of the *Seattle Times*, "The most virulent

BATTLESHIPS AT PUGET SOUND NAVY YARD, BREMERTON, WASHINGTON—There is room enough and depth enough to hold all the navies of the world.

This vintage photograph shows the Bremerton shipyard where the ghosts of war victims come and go in the big gray ships. (author's collection)

pandemic in world history probably slipped into Washington on September 17, 1918, when feverish naval recruits from Philadelphia docked at Bremerton's Puget Sound Naval Shipyard."

Dietrich goes on to say that despite the fact that nearly two hundred Washington servicemen were stricken by the flu that was already amassing fatalities on the East Coast, the army refused to cancel an event where ten thousand civilians would be exposed to the flu as they watched a review of the National Guard infantry. As a result, the deadly bug soon "began flashing through the civilian population like wildfire."

The flu. Heart attacks. Torpedoes, courtesy of past enemies.

They've all snatched precious life from those who have moved through Bremerton's historic shipyard. And most likely, a variety of deaths have left ghosts behind there. The majority would be those enlisted in the navy, proud to serve America. They may be so proud that they are not yet ready to leave their time and place of perceived glory and are simply clinging to the site where the giant gray ships still come and go.

Where Is My Head?

Dan Gallagher and his family will never forget the unusual roommate who shared their home in Watertown, Massachusetts. Built in 1750, the house has been remodeled many times over the years, but the basement has remained in original condition, Dan explained in the beginning of a letter to me. He continued:

> *We had a number of incidents take place while we were living there. The toaster oven in the kitchen would turn on by itself, and unseen hands snatched the headphones off of my daughter's head while she was riding her exercise bicycle in the downstairs area near our kitchen.*
>
> *I've seen shadows pass along the wall during the evening hours when all the lighting was steady. And my wife saw a headless soldier!*

The headless figure, in uniform, walked with a limp through the gate to the backyard. He walked around to our back door and paused, as if he was asking for help. After a few moments, the figure walked through the back door and into the house.

After hearing my wife's description of the soldier's uniform, I did a little research and discovered he was more than likely a Hessian soldier. We theorize that he must have been wounded and looking for medical help when he appeared at the back door of the house. The occupant of the house must have taken him in and helped him. The soldier would obviously have had his head at the time, so I figure that perhaps he was later killed and lost his head. The help he received at the house must have imprinted itself upon him so that his ghost returned to that spot.

The kitchen is located directly above the basement, and my wife always said she felt as if the energy from the manifestations was coming from down there. I know that we rarely went into the basement, except to do the laundry. Even then, we headed back upstairs as quickly as we could! There was a boarded-up recessed area in the basement, and I was unable to figure out its purpose. Perhaps there is a connection between that area and the haunting.

While Dan Gallagher makes an interesting point about a possible injury that caused the soldier to lose his head, the ghost's presentation may have nothing to do with his appearance upon death.

Ghosts often appear with missing parts. One theory says that they are simply unable to exert the energy necessary to present a full image.

When it comes to apparitions with missing parts, witnesses most commonly report that the apparitions are missing their lower extremities.

𝕲𝖍𝖔𝖘𝖙𝖘 𝖎𝖓 𝖙𝖍𝖊 𝕹𝖊𝖜𝖘

Graveyard Party

IN WILLISTON, TENNESSEE, an antebellum home that was once part of the historic Walker Plantation is today home to a small family and to the ghosts of Civil War soldiers buried on the grounds. The lovely home with its columned front porch was built in 1857 and was home to the slave-owning Walker family, one of the first families to settle in Williston.

Phantom conversations were first heard by a painter who was working during remodeling. Before long, the family, too, heard the jumbled voices, always sounding as if they came from the next room. "It sounds like someone is having a party," one family member told a reporter at the *Fayette County Review*.

It was common in the area for Confederate soldiers to be buried in shallow graves and under houses during the Civil War, and some believe it is the restless spirits of fatally wounded soldiers who haunt the home.

Where the **Dead** Wander

Gettysburg, Pennsylvania, is home to one of the most famous haunted battle sites in America. It was the biggest and bloodiest battle of the Civil War with over 51,000 soldiers killed. The horror filled the first three days of July 1863 and ended with the Union Army claiming victory over the Confederate troops.

What was once just a small town fifty miles northwest of Baltimore is today a major tourist magnet. Two million people visit the Gettysburg National Military Park each year to explore the twenty-six miles of park roads and scrutinize the fourteen hundred monuments. Whether they are looking for ghosts or not, countless visitors come away with inexplicable images on their photos and thrilling accounts of spirit encounters.

Apparitions of soldiers are most frequently witnessed. Sometimes the images are filmy and transparent. Other times they appear so solid that they are assumed to be live people dressed in period costume—until they vanish before astonished viewers' eyes!

Sometimes the soldiers float by without legs. A headless soldier on a ghostly horse is among the specters seen.

Downtown Gettysburg, about a mile north of the park, is also swarming with ghosts.

Built as the Hotel Gettysburg in 1890, one old inn took over the site of a 1797 tavern. Despite the newer structure, spirits of the Civil War seem rooted to the spot, for they are often seen at the hotel.

Hotel staff has named one ghost Rachel. Several times each year, guests report an eerie visit from the specter of a nurse who appears with a whoosh of cool air.

Some insist that she has communicated with them. She is distraught, they say, because of her inability to treat the many wounded soldiers with such horribly damaged limbs.

Nurse Rachel recently visited the same room twice, encountering a different startled guest each time. Both guests reported that their dresser drawers mysteriously popped open, and their clothing was yanked out.

Maybe Rachel simply wanted something to rip up into bandages. Like so many visitors to Gettysburg, Rachel, too, may see the bloodied apparitions of the wounded. It's only natural that she wants to help.

GETTYSBURG NATIONAL MILITARY PARK
97 Taneytown Road
Gettysburg, PA 17325
(717) 334-1124

THE BEST WESTERN GETTYSBURG HOTEL
One Lincoln Square
Gettysburg, PA 17325
(717) 337-2000

Friendly Fire

When employees of the museum in Fort Monroe, Virginia, are asked about the ghosts, they reply, "We are not supposed to talk about it."

The fort, named for United States President James Monroe, was completed in 1834 and is surrounded by a moat. Still an active army post, the stone fort is situated on the tip of the Virginia Peninsula on the Chesapeake Bay.

Despite the authorities' orders to keep the ghost stories quiet, the accounts still circulate. Some say that the tall, thin specter of Abraham Lincoln has been spotted in the officers' quarters. Others claim to have seen a woman in a gauzy white dress floating through part of the fort so haunted that it is known as "Ghost Alley."

Throughout the area, mysterious laughter is sometimes heard, and objects inexplicably vanish.

This vintage image of Fort Monroe, Virginia, was photographed around 1913. (author's collection)

An antique postcard depicts the entry to haunted Fort Monroe, Virginia. (author's collection)

It is possible that some of the fort's ghosts remain earthbound because of a tragedy a century ago. It was July 22, 1910, when the wives and children of artillerymen were invited to watch target practice. The men were instructed to pretend an imaginary fleet was passing the fort on the way to Washington.

It was to be the grandest target practice to date, but fate had an ugly plan.

As family members looked on, a powder charge exploded, blowing a few of the men to bits. Eleven were killed, and many others injured.

After such a devastating accident, it is no wonder that Fort Monroe is haunted.

69th. Co, No. 1. Gun Section, Ft. Monroe, Va.

PUBLISHED BY L. M. BROWN, PHOEBUS, VA.

*The above picture shows the men who were actually in the gun pit at the time of the accident at Fort Monroe, July 21st, 1910. Those with a * before their names were killed. No. 1 Robinson, 2 Thomas, 3 Davenport, 4 *Duffy, 5 Hoffman, 6 Raney, 7 Summer, 8 *Smith, 9 Gleason, 10 Humphreys, 11 *Sullivan, 12 Kennedy, 13 Sulzberger, 14 Newsom, 15 *Adie, 16 *Chadwick, 17 Brinkley, 18 *King, 19 *Hogan, 20 *Hess, 21 *Bradford, 22 *Turner, 23 Clement. Atkins killed, not in picture.*

This rare postcard shows a group of men shortly before many were killed in a horrific accident at Fort Monroe, Virginia, in 1910. (author's collection)

𝔊𝔥𝔬𝔰𝔱𝔰 𝔦𝔫 𝔱𝔥𝔢 𝔑𝔢𝔴𝔰

No Bones about It

THE DISCOVERY OF a Civil War skeleton sheds light on the spooky happenings at a Texas library, according to the August 21, 2004, issue of the *El Paso Times*.

Employees of the El Paso Library have seen two specters: a tall man they call "the captain" and a woman dubbed "the nurse." The apparitions materialize in a storage area in the library's sub-basement, twenty feet underground.

While digging in a site behind the library, workers recently unearthed an old skeleton believed to be a soldier, because the area was a military graveyard in the 1860s. Though the cemetery was later relocated, a few skeletons—and perhaps their ghosts—were left behind. Another skeleton was dug up during work on sewer lines in 1998.

Items move on their own, odd noises interrupt the peace, and water faucets turn themselves on at the library, according to the report. Longtime employee Terri Grant told reporter Daniel Borunda that an invisible presence once shoved her while she was investigating a noisy ruckus in a vacant section of the library. "I was not scared enough to quit," she said.

seven

Afraid of the Light

"When killers die, they never remain as ghosts."

When the speaker made that bold statement, no one in the audience challenged him. I, however, wanted to leap from my chair and protest. But I had already finished giving my talk, and it was his turn to speak.

We were at a paranormal conference, and I was listening to the session taught by one of my peers, a man well-respected in the field.

I bit my lip, wondering how he could know such a thing. He possesses no special powers. He can't know any more about the other side than the rest of us. He confirmed my contention that the term "ghost expert" is an oxymoron.

By their very nature, ghosts are mysterious and elusive beings. Out of reach and seldom seen, their secrets are hidden in the fleeting shadows.

We can collect witness accounts, measure energy levels in haunted sites, record ethereal voices on tape, and capture images on film.

When psychics scrutinize the afterlife, they sometimes provide explicit details about ghosts, but even their insights aren't certainties. We can study phenomena around a haunting but still have more questions than answers. I suspect that the only real ghost experts are ghosts themselves.

Though I held my tongue and did not contradict my fellow speaker, I and other ghost researchers have thick files on hauntings by killers.

I wonder if the evil ones remain earthbound for the same reasons as the innocent. Are they confused or shocked or simply attached to this plane? Maybe murderers have an entirely different reason for staying.

Maybe it is guilt.

If conscience does not nibble at them in life, perhaps fear does in death. Are these stuck souls afraid to meet their maker? Perhaps when they were made of flesh and bone they dismissed the "afterlife" as a fairy tale.

Smug in the belief that judgment day would never arrive, they committed their crimes, hurting others for their own gain. What happens when death curls its cold fingers around a murderer? How does a killer react to finding himself without a body?

Psychics and those who have had near-death experiences tell us of a brilliant light. To go to it, they say, is to be embraced by love. Does this same light shine for evil people? Does it offer them the same love?

Maybe. Maybe not.

This uncertainty could prompt a killer to turn away from the light, choosing instead to cower in the darkness.

Most of us take comfort in stories of a peaceful light where our dead loved ones are waiting to greet us. But what if the dead ones waiting for you are your victims? Killers might not be anxious for such a reunion.

When I imagine the heartless wraiths wandering the blackness of the despair they created, I muster a drop of pity for these wretched souls who are afraid of the light. Here are their stories.

"See Ya"

Warren Bridge was a man filled with hate.

His life of crime began when he became a burglar at age fifteen. At age nineteen on February 10, 1980, he and his accomplice, Robert Costa, walked into a Galveston, Texas, convenience store. As they robbed the store, Warren pointed his .38 pistol at the clerk, sixty-two-year-old Walter Rose, and pulled the trigger, shooting him four times.

It was a painful battle between life and death for the victim, who died two weeks later, four days after the robbers were arrested in a drug raid on their motel room.

Prison did not end Warren's violent streak. Filled with anger, the young Caucasian racist proudly displayed a tattoo of a Confederate flag. His assaults on black prisoners landed him in more trouble.

Despite the fact that Warren Bridge was sentenced to die, defense attorneys fought for his life and warded off the execution until November 23, 1994, when he was fed his last meal. He ate a double-meat cheeseburger, fish sticks, and peaches, and then was killed by lethal injection.

Before he died, he nodded toward his stepfather and said, "See ya."

Warren had plenty of time to contemplate his death and say goodbye to his family. He once said, "I don't want to be hanged or ride old Sparky. I'm not very fond of electricity. Just a plain bullet is cleaner somehow."

Walter Rose was given no choice. He did not get to pick a last meal or say long good-byes to his family. Warren Bridge took all of that away.

I must admit it is hard to not be angry as I write about Warren Bridge. I don't want to think of the killer stepping into the afterlife, free to roam. But because I received a letter from a woman who knew him well, I must entertain the idea.

Prison Guard Lorie Hopper tried not to think about the evil committed by the inmates she watched. "I treated everyone with respect," she confided. And the prisoners seemed to respect her for that.

It was not, after all, her job to punish the men on death row. They were human beings who had made mistakes, and their fate was in the hands of the law.

In her letter to me, Lorie wrote about her strange experience in 1994:

> *After staying home sick from work one November evening, I woke abruptly on the couch with the distinct feeling someone had just leaned over me, kissed my forehead and whispered, "Thank you."*
>
> *While I did not SEE anyone, there are some things that you just KNOW, and I KNEW that someone had been there.*
>
> *It was not a frightening experience. Just baffling. WHO was it?*
>
> *My first thought, naturally, was that it must have been my boyfriend. Unfortunately, he was sound asleep in our bedroom. Since we had argued earlier that evening, the "thank you" made no sense.*
>
> *When I returned to work the next day, I learned that while I was off work, an inmate had been executed. While I had previously known that Warren Bridge's execution was scheduled, it did not cross my mind until that moment that HE might have been my mystery visitor.*
>
> *Several months later, I finally told my strange story to another officer, and I almost fell over when she told me she had experienced the same thing on the same night.*

If Warren Bridge did indeed visit his prison guards after his execution, it may have been just the first stop on a long road.

In addition to those he had to thank, there were many waiting for his apologies.

The **Last** Resort

Are killers born or are they made? It is a huge question with no definitive answer, though experts find that a combination of the wrong genes and a traumatic childhood are usually factors when a person is without conscience.

On February 29, 1956, a killer was born in Rochester, Michigan, though when nurses peered at the wrinkled newborn, they saw only a baby girl. Aileen Carol Pittman never knew the man who provided half her genes. Her father, child molester Leo Dale Pittman, hung himself in prison in 1969. Aileen's troubled teenaged mother abandoned her, leaving allegedly abusive grandparents to raise her.

A bad seed planted in poisoned earth, Aileen became a thief, a prostitute, and a murderer. In fact, Aileen Wuronos has been immortalized in books and movies, because she is not the typical female serial killer. Unlike other women killers who most often murder with poison, Aileen shot her seven male victims.

Parts of the blockbuster movie *Monster*, starring Charlize Theron as the killer, were filmed in the Last Resort bar, Aileen's hangout. Al Bulling, owner of the bar, played himself in the movie. He thinks that Aileen favored his tavern because of its proximity to a pawnshop where she sold the valuables that she stole from her victims.

Al, who has owned the biker bar south of Daytona Beach, Florida, for two and a half decades, had felt a little sorry for the woman, who usually didn't have a place to go when the bar closed down for the night. He often let her sleep in a trailer out behind the bar.

Much of Aileen's saga had centered on the tavern, including her arrest. In January 1991, undercover officers posed as bikers and lured the killer out the front door of the bar, where she was surrounded by police.

Aileen's execution on October 9, 2002, has not stopped her from visiting the Last Resort. "She's still here," Al told me, explaining that she made her presence known moments after her death, when the bar was crowded with reporters who had gathered there to watch news of the execution on TV. A tub of knives suddenly leapt off of a shelf as startled witnesses gasped.

"She always said that she would be back," said Al.

Bartender Kelley Pleis told me that she, too, has experienced odd things at the bar, such as the quiet afternoon she was alone there. "Business had been slow, so I was reading," she said. Suddenly, the jukebox turned itself on. "It came on full blast," she said. "There was no explanation for it."

Eeriest of all are the breezeless days when the back door suddenly bursts open. As Al watches and waits, the hairs on the back of his arms stand at attention. He knows what is coming. The television suddenly switches channels, and then in the seconds it takes the invisible presence to walk across the room, the front door abruptly opens.

It is as if Aileen Wuornos is walking the path she walked in the days she camped out back.

Whenever the presence bursts through the back door, Al tries to remain nonchalant. As Aileen's unseen hands change the TV channels, Al asks, "Who pissed you off this time, Aileen?"

𝕲𝖍𝖔𝖘𝖙𝖘 𝖎𝖓 𝖙𝖍𝖊 𝕹𝖊𝖜𝖘

Ghostly Hostess

THE GHOST OF RUTH ELLIS has been seen walking through a locked door in Caesars nightclub in Streatham, London, according to the November 4, 2005, edition of the *Streatham Guardian.*

Ruth was a petite 103 pounds, mother of two, and just twenty-eight years old. She was also a convicted murderer and the last woman to be executed in the United Kingdom. She shot and killed her boyfriend, David Blakely, twenty-five, in the parking lot outside of a pub on Easter Sunday 1955.

Ruth and David had a tumultuous relationship, marked by jealously and abuse. The judicial process was swift, and Ruth was executed three months after an off-duty officer found her standing over David with a smoking gun in her hand. Hanged at Holloway Prison, her body was buried there, but her spirit apparently broke free, returning to a place with more innocent memories.

Her haunting of Caesars has the staff rattled. Club owner Fred Batt told a reporter, "I've heard a scream and so have members of my staff. It's very loud and high-pitched. I shivered the first time I heard it."

Ruth Ellis worked as a hostess in the building in 1946 when the place was called The Locarno. Today, employees refuse to set foot in the spookier area of the building. Batt told a reporter, "Even I won't go into the club by myself."

Locked Inside the Gray

Prisons are another place where killers roam decades after their flesh has turned to dust. Many haunted prisons no longer cage inmates. They have been turned into museums, where tourists wander freely from cell to tiny cell and try to imagine what it must have been like to be locked inside the gray.

The cold steel doors stand open, and the heavy keys are simply interesting relics. Yet those who were once trapped sometimes remain. It is as if they don't see the way out. Both the guilty and the innocent linger behind the bars of the following prisons and jails.

Deadly Silence

When the Quakers thought up a unique way of rehabilitating inmates, they certainly did not imagine that their tactics would drive the prisoners insane. A peaceful people, they believed that their methods would send criminals along the right path. Put a man in an isolated cell, they figured, and he would have plenty of time to contemplate his wrongdoing.

To accomplish complete isolation, they built the Eastern State Penitentiary in Philadelphia in the early nineteenth century with a modern feature that even the White House did not yet enjoy—private flushing toilets. There would be no camaraderie in a common restroom, no "good morning" or, "Please pass the toilet paper."

Each cell had its own toilet, so there was no need to venture out.

Meals were delivered by unseen attendants who slid the trays beneath the cold doors with never a word spoken. The isolation was indeed complete.

A few lucky prisoners captured mice to tame for pets. Everyone else was all alone.

The suffering began on October 25, 1829, when the first inmate entered the castle-like structure. In addition to the loneliness, prisoners endured cruel punishment at the direction of Warden Samuel Wood.

Lonely prisoners lived long, sad lives in total isolation at Eastern State Pen. (Leslie Rule)

Every nook and cranny of the Eastern State Penitentiary hides secrets. (Leslie Rule)

The tiny padlock on this old door could not have stopped the tough men once housed at Eastern State Penitentiary. (Leslie Rule)

top: Tour guides of Eastern State Penitentiary shiver at the sound of evil cackling here. (Leslie Rule)
above: Eastern State Penitentiary, once known as Cherry Hill, was a formidable prison that drove the toughest men to tears. (Leslie Rule)

Inmates who were caught making noise were led outside in freezing temperatures, stripped naked, and doused with ice water.

In 1833, prisoner Matthias Maccumsey was punished with the iron gag. The horrible contraption of iron and chains was inserted into his mouth and fastened so tightly that if he moved just slightly, he would suffer unbearable pain. Though the device was not designed to be fatal, it killed Matthias.

Inmates, desperate to escape, dug tunnels, scaled walls, and swam through rat-infested sewers. In 1925, prisoner James Gordon escaped by hiding in a truck full of hot ashes. He was free for a year before being apprehended in Los Angeles.

When infamous gangster Al Capone was jailed at Eastern, he claimed that the specter of James Clark haunted him. Shot and killed during Chicago's black Valentine's Day Massacre, the angry ghost apparently blamed Al, who could be heard shrieking, "Leave me alone!"

When I visited the prison-turned-museum, employees told me that they've seen shadowy figures darting in and out of the cells. The most haunted area, they said, are the cells where the meanest criminals

Statues of the white cats that once roamed the old prison grounds of Eastern State Penitentiary are placed throughout the popular tourist attraction. (Leslie Rule)

were housed. When witnesses hear evil cackling emanating from the dense stone walls, they don't stick around to see who is laughing.

EASTERN STATE PENITENTIARY

2124 Fairmount Avenue

Philadelphia, PA 19130

(215) 236-3300

www.easternstate.org

The Rock

Alcatraz is widely acclaimed as a haunted island. "The Rock" is today a tourist destination for those visiting San Francisco and is most famous for its past as a prison for hard-core criminals.

Paranormal investigator Mollie Stewart discovered a range of ghostly activity there. Unseen hands open and shut the doors to cells, and the eerie sound of a harmonica floats from nowhere. "It is an extremely haunted site," she said.

While many witnesses believe the earthbound spirits belong to the killers once imprisoned there, they are not aware of a tragic episode that occurred on the island long before it caged the worst of the worst.

At one time, the island was a military base, and it was during this era when a sad human drama played out. While scrutinizing newspaper archives, I unearthed a skeleton that was buried so long ago that it has been forgotten.

Surgeon William Dietz was a captain in the military who lived on the island with his wife, Ella, and their child. On January 28, 1891, Captain Deitz did something terrible. He shot and killed his wife and then turned the rifle on himself, leaving his eight-year-old an orphan. The horrific murder-suicide certainly accounts for some of the paranormal activity at Alcatraz.

Alcatraz is an island in the San Francisco Bay
Ferries leave from Pier 41

FISHERMAN'S WHARF
San Francisco, CA
Tickets: (415) 705-5555
www.nps.gov/alcatraz/

Deadly Redemption

Recognizable to movie fans as the set for *The Shawshank Redemption* and many other films, the Ohio State Reformatory in Mansfield was filled with drama long before actors such as Tim Robbins ever set foot on the gloomy grounds.

Since the Ohio prison opened in 1896, its impenetrable walls have witnessed suicides, deadly prison breaks, riots, and horrible accidents.

The real-life haunted prison is turned into a staged haunted prison during Halloween season. Actors play ghostly killers, strategically placed lights casts eerie shadows, and spooky sounds emanate from cobwebbed corners. But sometimes it is hard to tell what is pretend and what is real, for the screaming continues after the actors have gone home, the special effects are turned off, and the place is buttoned up for the night.

A scent of flowery perfume wafts from nowhere on the third floor of the administration building. Staff credit it to the gentle spirit of Helen Glattke, who once lived on the prison grounds with her husband, Chief Arthur Glattke.

Poor Helen met her fate on a quiet Sunday morning in November 1950. According to November 7 editions of Ohio newspapers, the forty-one-year-old mother of two was getting dressed when she reached up on a high shelf for her jewelry box. Helen's fingers curled around her husband's .32-caliber automatic pistol, a defective weapon that often jammed. This morning it was in her way, and as she tried to move it, it slipped from her grasp, discharging as it fell.

A bullet pierced her left upper lung, and she later died at General Hospital. The saddest thing of all was that she did not get to see nine-year-old Teddy and thirteen-year-old Arthur Jr. grow up. It is somehow comforting to know that her spirit is sensed in the administration building and not in the shadowy places where the evil wraiths roam.

Some say they have witnessed Helen's shadowy shape and even felt her soft touch as she caresses their faces and shoulders.

OHIO STATE REFORMATORY

100 Reformatory Road

Mansfield, OH 44905

(419) 522-2644

www.mrps.org

Haunted Cage

A former warehouse turned museum in London, England, seems to be brimming with restless ghosts. After employees experienced phenomena there, the Paranormal Search and Investigation team checked it out, and both their psychics and their electronic equipment picked up on entities.

A hostile energy on the third floor near the gibbet cage spooked the group. The gibbet cage was used to display the dead bodies of pirates in the 1700s. The lawbreakers' lives of plundering and violence came to an end when they were captured and hung on Execution Dock in Wapping, a section of London.

The grisly sight of the executed pirates was meant to serve as a warning to others who might be tempted to become outlaws of the sea.

While the bodies of the dead pirates are dust in the wind, their angry souls apparently still cling to the cage that showcased their public humiliation.

MUSEUM IN DOCKLANDS
Canary Wharf
West India Quay
London, England E14 4AL
www.museumindocklands.org.uk/English/

Hanging Out

The Frontenac County Courthouse in Kingston, Ontario, is a formidable yet elegant structure. With its grand entry of towering columns and domed tower, the historic gray building draws the eyes of passersby. Originally constructed in 1796, it suffered fire damage twice and each time was rebuilt. During one renovation, workers discovered a clue to the strange goings-on there.

Over the years witnesses had reported seeing a peculiar man. He was always leaning against the same courthouse wall. A noose hung from his neck, and before observers could question why, the figure vanished.

Six sanctioned hangings had occurred at the Frontenac County Courthouse and Jail—the first in December of 1867 and the last in January of 1949.

Apparently, an unauthorized execution was also conducted there. Construction workers discovered a grisly surprise when they cut through the very wall where the apparition had been sighted.

Hidden behind the wall was a skeleton in a makeshift coffin. His identity remains a mystery. Once he was given a proper burial, sightings of his ghost ceased.

FRONTENAC COUNTY COURTHOUSE
5 Court Street
Kingston, Ontario K7L 2N4

Ghosts in the News

Those in Glass Houses

THE BODMIN JAIL in Cornwall, England, is home to an eerie presence, according to an April 6, 2005, report from the *BBC News*. Erected in 1776, the castle-like jail was the site of more than fifty-five executions. More than twenty thousand spectators turned out to watch one public hanging. The last prisoner was hanged in 1909, and apparently he and some of his peers are still around.

When members of the Paranormal Site Investigators (PSI) spent the night in Bodmin Jail, two of the team were overcome by inexplicable nausea that drove them from the building, said the *BBC News* report. When the members were exploring the gloomy underground cells, stones were tossed at them by an unseen source. The mystery of the stones was deepened when it was discovered there were no nearby windows, and the ceiling was made of metal. The rocks apparently materialized from the other side and were "significantly hotter than the ambient temperature of the cell, the roof, and the floor."

Team leader Nicky Sewell, who managed to get a tape recording of a ghostly grunt, told a reporter, "There's definitely something at Bodmin Jail which was trying to make its presence known to us that night."

eight

Stranger Than Fiction

Actress Sharon Tate was one of "the beautiful people." It was a fact that annoyed Charles Manson, the wild-eyed monster who orchestrated a mass murder that shocked America on August 9, 1969. A sociopath who could charm the last vestige of integrity out of a lost soul, Manson had followers. They were a confused group of young hippies known as his "family."

Set on destroying those who achieved wealth, he targeted Sharon's home in Bel Air, California, and directed his followers to savagely kill its five occupants and to write words from The Beatles' songs on the walls in blood.

Sharon, a lovely blond actress famous for her role as Jennifer North in *Valley of the Dolls,* was eight months pregnant when she was murdered.

Mercifully, Sharon's younger sister was not in the house that night. She had asked if she could spend the night, but her big sister had said no, that she was too tired for company.

I've often wondered if she had had a premonition that it would not be safe for her little sister and had used fatigue as an excuse.

According to a story that has been circulating for decades, Sharon had had a strange premonition long before the tragic night. While the anecdote has changed over the years as it is told and retold, the earliest version is probably closest to the truth.

Standing at the top of a staircase, Sharon glanced down to see an apparition of herself murdered at the foot of the stairs.

It is not the first time I have heard of ghosts appearing out of our timeline. When it comes to their realm, they do not seem to have the rules that confine us in our world. While Tuesday never comes before Monday on this side, events may be haphazard and out of sequence in theirs.

I experienced this sort of ghostly time warp in 1982. I was walking along Kent–Des Moines Road, in Des Moines, Washington. The normally busy stretch of curving road was unnaturally still, when I heard a pitiful scream.

I turned to see a blond woman standing on the balcony of an apartment in a large complex. She had a little girl about six or seven by the ankles and was dangling her in the air, two stories above the ground. I could not see the child's face, because she was facing inward.

Her long blond hair rippled in the breeze as she shrieked. In shock, I rushed to the apartment manager's office, and as I opened my mouth to ask her to phone the police, I began to cry instead. The emotion of witnessing the scene had overwhelmed me to where my lips could barely form words.

A policewoman responded, but when she visited the apartment in question, she was told that there was no one there who matched my description.

I knew what I had seen and assumed that the residents were lying to protect an abusive friend who had left in a hurry with the young victim in tow. When I described the incident to my mother, however, she gently said, "I think you saw a ghost."

I dismissed the idea. I could not believe that ghosts could appear so solid. This had been real. The event occurred years before I began researching ghosts, and despite my other paranormal experiences, I was skeptical.

I will never forget the surreal quality of the scene. The child's scream had sounded tinny, almost as if it were echoing from the bottom of a big tin can. And the emotion I'd felt was nearly too much to handle.

Several years later, I was sitting in court in Eugene, Oregon, assisting my mother in researching her second true crime book, *Small Sacrifices*.

Diane Downs, a letter carrier with an obsession for a married man who did not want children, was accused of shooting her three children as they slept in her car on a lonely stretch of country road.

Nine-year-old Christy and four-year-old Danny survived the shooting, but poor little Cheryl, age seven, was killed.

I could not remember the face of the abusive mother on the balcony, but the slender figure and the blond hairstyle matched Diane's. The frail ghostly child's long hair looked exactly like Cheryl's.

Did I, perhaps, see what was happening to poor Cheryl as it occurred? Or was I witnessing a future event? I do not know if Diane ever actually dangled her sad middle child from a balcony.

If, indeed, the scene on the balcony was of a paranormal nature and connected to the Downs child's murder, why did I see them? The murder happened in Oregon, and I witnessed the scene in Washington, long before the homicide.

Why me?

Emotion.

We find that emotion plays a huge role in psychic phenomena. My very presence at the trial tied me emotionally to Cheryl. I, like some others who covered the trial, suffered from anxiety throughout, as I tried to wrap my mind around the idea that a mother could kill her child.

Several years after Diane Downs was convicted, a movie was made based on my mother's book. It starred Farrah Fawcett, and my mother and I were extras in the movie, sitting in the courtroom where we had in real life. I covered the making of the film for a Sunday feature in the *Oregonian*, the major newspaper in Portland, Oregon.

Though it was admittedly exciting to be involved in the making of a movie and to pen my first big article, icy fingers of dread sometimes twisted my stomach into knots so tight I was physically ill.

When talented Farrah, made up to appear pregnant, sat at the defense

table for her courtroom scenes, I flashed on the memory of Diane Downs in the real-life scene.

I will never forget the sight of Diane with her smug smile, as she continuously ran the tips of her fingers over her huge pregnant belly. She was growing another child, she maintained, so she would have someone to love her.

top: Farrah Fawcett played the deadly mother in the ABC miniseries *Small Sacrifices*, based on Ann Rule's book. Was the ghost of an abused child I spotted one shocking afternoon connected to the case? (Leslie Rule)
above: Farrah Fawcett on the set with John Shea, who played the prosecutor who put Diane Downs behind bars. (Leslie Rule)

My mother and I still think of little Cheryl, the pitiful middle child who never stood a chance. And when I think of the shrieking girl I saw dangled from the balcony, I feel a coldness that goes to my toes. If that child was the out of time ghost of Cheryl, it was an occurrence stranger than fiction.

Read on for more ghostly accounts too strange for fiction.

Marvelous Marvin

When I research and write about the paranormal, I never intend to include myself in the stories. Yet, when peculiar things happen to me, I am torn. On the one hand, I am self-conscious about sharing. *What if readers think that I am nuts?*

On the other hand, I feel that I am cheating my readers if I do not share my own experiences. Without the many people who shared their strange stories with me, I could not write ghost books.

It seems only fair that I also confide.

At the time I wrote the previous page, I had yet to experience the odd thing that I am about to confess. In fact, it occurred last night, and as I write these words, I am on the plane, returning from a research trip to Reno, Nevada.

I was invited to Nevada by fellow ghost author Janice Oberding, who assured me that the state was so haunted that there were enough ghost stories for both of us.

Janice and her friends, electronic voice phenomena (EVP) experts Mark and Debby Constantino, had read my books and were eager to meet me and escort me to some of their favorite haunted spots.

Mark and Debby are pioneers in the exploration of a phenomenon that is all at once exciting, baffling, and chilling. While EVP is not yet a common household term, it soon will be.

An EVP is the mysterious presence of a voice on tape. Investigators throughout the world are taping voices that seem to belong to the dead. Though ghostly voices can be recorded with any ordinary tape recorder or answering machine, researchers like the Constantinos have learned to utilize this equipment to maximize the results.

When they visit haunted locations, the husband and wife team turn on a voice-activated tape recorder and take turns asking questions posed to whatever entity is within earshot. They then wait for a full ten seconds to give ghosts plenty of time to respond. Sometimes one of the team will generate white noise, such as that of a small hand-held, battery-operated fan. They wait, the fan whirring softly as ten seconds drift by.

As Debby explains it, the white noise is a sort of raw material, akin to a sculptor's slab of clay. While the sculptor can turn an indefinable lump of clay into a magnificent bust, the ghosts can take the whir of a fan and mold the sound into words, complete with distinctive voices, inflections, and accents.

Though the voices are rarely heard during the actual recording, they are inexplicably on the tape when it is rewound and played.

Debby and Mark were excited about sharing their most impressive EVPs with me. The clearest voice they had ever gotten, they told me, was without white noise. Not only that, it was in their own home. The fact that Debby is very psychic likely adds to the couple's success in obtaining so many phantom voices on tape.

In February of 2005, they were experimenting with collecting EVPs in their home when they received an unprecedented number of replies. The phenomena continued for forty-eight hours, prompting the couple to stay awake the entire time.

When Mark went to the store, Debby left the voice-activated recorder on the dining room table and stepped into the kitchen to tidy up.

As she bustled about, she heard a cat meowing in an extremely expressive manner. She assumed it was their cat, Wheezy, prowling about the dining room, and she wondered vaguely why the kitty was so excited.

But was the meowing she heard really that of her cat?

Janice Oberding and her husband, Bill, and I all sat on the Constantinos' huge, comfortable couch and listened as they played their favorite EVPs.

"The woman's voice is really clear on this one," said Mark, as he brought up another file on his laptop computer. It was the EVP obtained the day Debby was in the kitchen, when her kitty meowed in such an odd manner. The EVP began with a long string of meows that was presumably the voice of their kitty, Wheezy.

The taped meows were followed by a mysterious adult male's voice, meowing back at the cat, in the playful manner that humans do. I listened with interest, but it was the next word spoken by a distinctive female voice that made me sit up straight. It was a single word, formed into a question.

"*Marvin?*"

I gasped. I knew the voice well. *It was my own.*

"That's me!" I exclaimed. "Play it again!"

I made them play it over and over again, and each time I heard it, I repeated in awe, "That's me!"

"It does sound like you," Janice agreed.

But how could it be? The recording was made thirteen months before I had met any of these people, before I had ever set foot in Reno.

"*Marvin?*"

It took a few moments for me to regain my composure enough to explain to my new friends the significance of Marvin.

None of them knew about the sadness I have carried daily since May 2005. They did not know about Marvin. Marvelous Marvin was my tuxedoed cat who was not quite two years old when I lost him. It is not something that I like to talk about, but it is with me always.

Normally an inside cat, Marvin's first taste of the wild may have been his last. A freak set of circumstances ended with me and my cats camping for several days on a friend's wooded acreage in Eatonville, Washington, in May 2005.

My animals are my only children, and it hurts to put these words down on paper. My cats were out of my sight, when I heard the horrible yips of a marauding pack of coyotes. I rushed to investigate, but the coyotes were gone, and so were Marvin, Piper Sam, and Frank.

My remaining cats stared at me, their eyes wide and concerned. But they could not tell me what had happened. I pray every day that the three missing cats were simply frightened away by the coyotes and have found new, wonderful homes.

Now, as I write about the ghosts of victims, I wonder if Marvin was the victim of the coyotes. Has my charismatic kitty become a subject in my book? Is he a spirit, sending me a message? Did Marvin somehow manifest my voice, so that I would know that the frantic meows were his?

I have no answers, but so many questions.

At the time that Debby obtained the EVP of the voice like mine, it was several months before the awful day I lost my cats.

Marvin, my amazing kitten, and I are working on a project called "A Kitten's Work Is Never Done." Marvin sews his own clothes. Marvin carefully hangs laundry in the little set I built for him and then yawns, exhausted from the work. Did Marvin communicate with me out of time and out of space from the other side? (Leslie Rule)

If Marvin's ghost did supply the cosmic meows on the EVP, how did he do it three months before he vanished?

As mentioned in the previous chapter, the theory that time is non-existent on the other side may apply here. Perhaps Marvin's spirit traveled to the best place possible to get a message to me.

If so, it was not the first time that Marvin took paranormal steps to telepathically communicate. In October 2004, I received a telephone call from a psychic whom I barely knew. She lived in California, and I had spoken to her only a couple of times when I interviewed her for a story.

She knew little about me. She knew that I had cats, but I had never described them to her. On the morning that she called, I had been worrying about Marvin. He was lethargic, and his eyes were runny.

"I had to call you," she told me. "One of your cats contacted me. He is black and white," she said, as she described the exact areas of Marvin's white markings. "He has a cold, and you need to take him to vet, but he will be OK."

I was stunned. How did she know?

"He is very persistent," she said.

I immediately took Marvin to the vet, and as the woman had predicted, he had a cold. He received medication and soon recovered.

Since Marvin went missing, I have wished many times that he would communicate with me as I close my eyes and imagine that I am holding him.

All three cats who disappeared were my beloved furry friends. Marvin, however, stood whiskers and tail above most felines. Unusually intelligent, he also was very loving to both people and other animals alike. I still hope that he is alive and well. I hope that the psychic messages he is sending are from this side and not the other. I am afraid, however, that Marvin is another murdered spirit.

When I met the Oberdings and the Constantinos, I felt immediately bonded with all of them. We are all big animal lovers and, coincidentally, had all lost beloved pets in the weeks prior. The Oberdings lost their geriatric black lab named, Buddy, and I lost my geriatric cat, also named Buddy. The Constantinos had lost three animals in the last year, including their cat, Wheezy, who had died just days before our meeting.

As it turned out, Debby had e-mailed me in the summer of 2005. She had seen the amazing photograph of the ghost cat, taken by an Oregon woman, in my book *Ghosts Among Us* and wanted to borrow the photo for a presentation she was giving at a paranormal conference.

My computer crashed, and all of my e-mail was lost before I could respond to her. When she told me that she had e-mailed me, I told her that I remembered her letter and apologized for not answering.

As Debby said, "There are no coincidences." The odd connection we shared that swirled around the life, death, and ghosts of pets was compelling.

As Debby and Mark finished their two-day marathon of recording phantom voices, they were exhausted and, apparently, the ghosts were too. One of the last EVPs they got before finally going to sleep was an exasperated male voice that said, "Enough, lady!"

To hear EVPs captured by the Constantinos, visit www.spirits-speak.com.

Little Boy Lost

It was a lovely October day in 2004 when Jason Sweeton visited Truckee, California. In the area on business, the clinical researcher for the Food and Drug Administration found himself with some spare time and decided to hike the trails at the Donner Memorial State Park. "It was the middle of the week and very quiet," he said, explaining that he passed a few folks on the path before finding himself alone in the forest.

Sunshine speckled the ground, scattered like gold coins in the shadows of the pine trees. The peace was so complete that he was acutely aware of the sharp crunch of gravel beneath his every step.

Jason knew that this was the site of an appalling tragedy a century and a half before. It was the spot where the ill-fated Donner Party had found itself snowed in and literally starving to death.

In a case that horrified the world, some of the malnourished pioneers had succumbed to cannibalism to survive. An exhibit and a monument to those who had suffered here was prominently displayed.

Jason had heard rumors the place was haunted, but he did not take them seriously. "I've never been interested in ghosts," he told me. "I'm typically a skeptical individual." He simply wanted to photograph the scenery to share with his wife, Jacqueline, who was home with their baby in their Round Rock, Texas, home. He took a number of shots with his digital camera and, after a relaxing hike, headed back to his hotel, where he scrolled through the photos.

Something caught his eye.

"It was the undeniable face of a child," he said.

The little face appeared in the bottom corner of a photo that Jason had taken of the tree-lined path. Ever-so-slightly blurred, as if the child had dashed in close for a peek at him, the colors on the image are real and distinct.

From the deep blue eyes to the varied tones

A visitor to the Donner Memorial Park was shocked by the image in the lower right-hand corner. (Jason Sweeton) of the flesh to the light brown hair highlighted in the sunlight, the image is as clear as any snapshot of a human being. While only the top of the head, one eye, and the rise of a tiny nose are in view, it is evident that the hair is short, like a boy's, and that his face is puffy with bags beneath the eyes.

Jason picked up the phone and called his wife.

Jacqueline remembers their conversation. "He was really freaked out," she said, as she recalled how he had tried to make sense of the anomaly. She told him that surely he would have noticed if there had been children running around.

Of course he would have.

The silence had practically screamed at him. He had definitely been alone there.

The practical-minded Jason, who has a degree in biology, stressed, "My job mandates that I observe with a critical mind." Yet, he cannot explain how the child appeared in the picture.

Since his paranormal surprise, Jason has read up on the Donner Party, but until I spoke with him, he had not heard about one particularly shocking death of a toddler.

Jeremiah George Foster was born on August 24, 1844, in St. Louis, Missouri. He was not quite two years old when he and his parents, William and Sarah, left Missouri in May 1846 with a group of folks headed by wagon train for a new life in California. Jeremiah's maternal grandmother, Levina Murphy, thirty-six, also accompanied them.

They joined a larger team and eventually camped beside the Little Sandy River in an area that is today part of Wyoming. As they sat around the campfire, the men debated about the best route to take. Some argued that a shortcut would get them to California quicker.

Instead of continuing with the large group on the known route, a new party was formed, with George Donner pronounced the leader. The Donner Party branched off from the others as they continued west.

Jeremiah and his family were among those in the unfortunate

assembly that did not foresee the suffering they would endure as they crossed the rugged terrain of mountains and seemingly endless deserts.

By the time they rejoined the California trail, their "shortcut" had cost them three precious weeks. In the Sierra Nevada, they were blanketed by a blinding snow, which stung their faces, froze their fingers, and blocked their path. Eighty-one people found themselves trapped in the mountains.

The group split up, with one cluster camping by a lakeside, and the other, six miles away by Alder Creek. The oxen were killed for food, but it was not enough to ward off starvation. People began to die. Faced with either death or survival, some turned to cannibalism.

While a few had forged ahead to look for help, others stayed behind. Jeremiah and his grandmother huddled in the Murphy Cabin beside the lake as they anxiously waited for Sarah and William's return.

The child's ribs were sharply outlined beneath his pale flesh, and he stared pleadingly at the adults. When Levina watched her grandson crying with hunger, it broke her heart. But there was nothing she could do to help him or the other little ones.

Among those at the Murphy Cabin was a man who has become a controversial figure. Survivors painted him as an abusive man, cruel to his wife and concerned only with himself.

Some of his descendants, however, are angry with this description and insist that their ancestor has been unfairly portrayed. They reject accusations that Lewis Keseberg developed a taste for human flesh.

Yet, many believe the alleged account of little Jeremiah's last night alive in March 1847. It was another bleak evening with no hope in sight when Lewis Keseberg insisted that the toddler sleep in his bed.

When Levina awoke in the morning, she was horrified to see her grandchild's limp body hanging on a hook on the wall. He had died during the night, Lewis Keseberg told her. Now, his flesh would sustain the others.

In shock, Levina accused him of murdering her grandson.

Perhaps Lewis Keseberg was innocent. He cannot, after all, defend himself, because he is no longer here.

And neither is little Jeremiah.

Or is he?

The small boy who appears in Jason Sweeton's photograph looks to be between two and four years old. Jeremiah was two and a half when he died. Other children perished, including three-year-old James Eddy, who succumbed after Jeremiah.

The little ghost could be any of the small ones, but if one believes that Jeremiah was murdered, then the spirit is probably his.

Jason Sweeton was walking toward the boulder that once served as a Murphy Cabin wall when he raised his camera and caught the ethereal image. His artistic eye was framing the snaking trail, flanked by sun-dappled trees. It is a calendar-quality photograph with an unexpected bonus.

Why did the little boy appear in Jason's photo? Could it be that the toddler is still waiting for his daddy and recognized the paternal energy in Jason?

It is sad to imagine hungry little ghosts still waiting for help. Jeremiah's devoted grandmother died weeks after he did. If he is still there, she, too, may be there, looking after him. It is a comforting thought.

DONNER MEMORIAL STATE PARK AND EMIGRANT TRAIL MUSEUM
12593 Donner Pass at Highway 80
Truckee, CA 96161
(530) 582-7892

Donner Party Ghosts

Jeremiah George Foster is not the only Donner Party victim to materialize in places where the pioneers camped. Inside the Emigrant Trail Museum, artifacts from the wagon trail days are on display.

A couple dressed in period clothing has been seen beside a wagon there. Visitors usually assume that they are actors, hired to add authenticity to the exhibit—until they suddenly vanish.

Apparitions are also seen outside of the museum.

"A ghost we believe to be Tamsin Donner has been seen by many people," said author and historian Janice Oberding, elaborating on the devoted mother's tragic ending.

Tamsin Donner was torn. While her children stayed at the Alder Creek camp, her ailing husband, sixty-two-year-old George, was six miles away at Murphy Cabin.

The determined woman trudged through the snow between the two areas, desperately trying to care for both her husband and children.

Tamsin, 45, died after George, and there was just one witness to her death.

Lewis Keseberg, the questionable character who some have accused of murder, claimed that Tamsin showed up at the Murphy Cabin in an unfortunate state.

She had fallen into the creek, he said. Soaking wet and disoriented, Tamsin babbled incoherently about how she needed to get back to her children.

When she died suddenly, Louis did not let her body go to waste. "It was the finest flesh I'd ever tasted," he allegedly commented.

"Tamsin's skeleton was never found," said Janice Oberding, who suspects that she is buried beside the Donner Party memorial rock, which once served as a wall of the Murphy Cabin.

If detectives were so inclined, they could unearth the remains of Tamsin so that modern forensics could determine the cause of death. A blow to the head or a strangling death may still be detectable.

If she was murdered, it may explain why she has been earthbound for so long. Her glowing figure still walks the path toward the Murphy Cabin.

The apparition of the woman in pioneer clothing materializes near the pioneer monument and floats toward the Emigrant Trail Museum.

"That is the path she took on her way to see her sick husband," explained Janice, as she pointed to the location of the long-ago trail.

Is Tamsin Donner reliving her last journey?

What really happened on that trail? Did she stumble into a stream, as Lewis maintained, and suffer from fatal hypothermia?

Or did she stumble upon something even more dangerous than icy cold water?

The answer is buried somewhere on the grounds of the Donner Memorial State Park.

Yet another Donner Party memorial is also believed to be home to ghosts of the tragic pioneers. "Not many people know about it," said Janice Oberding, who took me to see the plaque.

At the foot of Rattlesnake Mountain, the bronze plaque is situated between houses in a modern housing development in the Donner Springs neighborhood, a subdivision in Reno, Nevada.

It was here that the Donner Party camped during its last happy

This spot at the foot of Rattlesnake Mountain in Reno, Nevada, served as the campsite for the Donner Party before its members ventured onto dark trails. (Leslie Rule)

An enormous boulder once served as the wall of a cabin where members of the Donner Party took refuge. Today, a memorial plaque attached to the rock remembers both the victims and the survivors. Some believe human remains are buried at this spot. (Leslie Rule)

time. Though the members of the party were warned that the weather would soon change and that they should move quickly, they lingered. The children frolicked in the sunshine as the adults dreamed of the new life in California.

Do the restless ghosts of the Donner Party wander back to the spot where they last enjoyed the warmth of sunshine and the satisfaction of full bellies? (Leslie Rule)

"They stayed too long," said Janice.

By the time the group got moving, the mild season was running out of days. The mean winter weather crept in, its icy fists pummeling the pioneers with snow until their path was blocked. Some of the ghosts went back to the last place where life was good, theorizes Janice who once ran a tour of haunted places in Reno.

One night, about ten p.m. she led a bus full of tourists to the old campsite on Peckham Lane. As the folks wandered around exploring, the skeptical driver stayed in the bus.

He was friendly, and Janice liked him, but she couldn't help notice how he rolled his eyes as she told ghost stories to the eager group.

While Janice waited for her tourists to finish examining the place, the driver motioned to her from the doorway of the bus. "Don't tell the others," he whispered, "but I just saw a ghost!" His hand trembling, he raised his arm and pointed to the spot where he had seen a little girl in a white nightgown materialize.

She studied his face, wondering if he was teasing her, but he was genuinely shaken. "He didn't believe in ghosts before that," she said.

Janice smiled to herself. The bus driver was new to the state and had no idea that it was not the first time a nightgown-clad girl had been seen in the area.

A couple of years before, authorities were baffled when drivers reported seeing a child in a white nightgown near McCarran Boulevard. "It was in the dead of winter and on a cold night," remembered Janice, who had read the accounts in the newspaper.

The girl appeared to be three or four, too young to be wandering in the dark and cold. Several people reported seeing her, including one woman who said she approached the child.

But the little girl ran from the woman, disappearing into the night.

"They searched for her for days," said Janice, remembering how concerned people were.

It did not occur to the police that it could be too late to help the child. The authorities did not consider the possibility that the small girl had been dead for a century and a half.

If the evasive figure was indeed a spirit left behind by the Donner Party, it could have been Ava Keseberg, the three-year-old daughter of Lewis.

The little one perished on the trail as a group of folks forged ahead. After she died, they were unable to carry her with them and buried her in the snow.

A ghostly child in a white nightgown materializes here. (Leslie Rule)

Her father was unaware of her death until he was finally able to leave the area. When he saw a piece of fabric poking from the snow, he was curious and tugged on it. The snow fell away, and he found himself staring at poor little Ava.

Ava may still be trying to find her way back to her family.

The ghost, of course, could be any one of the small children who lost their lives that winter. Boys, too, wore nightgowns in that era and often had long hair.

Survivors of the Donner Party passed their stories along, each version shaded by their own perceptions. The passing years have surely distorted these accounts all the more. We cannot know what was in the hearts of those who walked the frozen trails.

The answers to the Donner Party mysteries are buried with the dead, their secrets unspoken on the lips of ghosts. Unless they speak up, we will never know what really transpired.

Speaking Up

On the snowy day that I visited the Donner Memorial State Park, I was accompanied by electronic voice phenomena experts Debby and Mark Constantino and ghost hunter Janice Oberding.

The Constantinos had brought along a tape recorder, and we took turns asking questions of whatever unseen beings might be present.

"Introduce yourselves first before you ask a question," Mark advised Janice and me, explaining that they always tried to be considerate of the earthbound spirits.

After each question, we were to wait a full ten seconds to give the ghosts plenty of time to respond.

"The tape recorder is voice activated," said Debby. "Even though we can't hear the ghosts, we know that they are speaking when the recorder is recording."

Sure enough, as we stood in the silence, we could see the indicator on the machine revealing that it was picking up some type of noise.

The Constantinos phoned me several days after I had returned home. They were in the middle of the time-consuming task of replaying the tapes and removing background noise. "We definitely got voices," Mark said.

top: Ghost researcher Janice Oberding points out the path where the ghost of Tamsin Donner travels. Mark and Debby Constantino prepare to attempt contact with the desperate spirit. The Constantinos are the authors of *Talking with Ghosts: A Step by Step Guide to Spirit Communication through EVP.* (Leslie Rule)
above: Mark Constantino records a question and then waits for a response from earthbound spirits of the Donner Party tragedy. (Leslie Rule)

"They are very quiet, though," said Debby. "Almost whispery."

"Did a Frank die there?" asked Mark. "We got a voice saying, 'Frank.'"

"Let me see," I said, as I leafed through the photographs I had taken of the site. I found a picture of the memorial plaque on the giant rock. It listed both survivors and victims. Among those who had perished were Franklin Graves Sr., fifty-seven, and Franklin Graves Jr., five.

The other remarks they recorded included the following:

"I'm hungry."

"Look for the bones."

"Please move."

And two simple words bothered us the most.

"Help us."

They **Creep** Up from Below

If there were ever a portal to the spirit realm, it is in my own backyard.

Seattle.

I came into the world here on a dark and stormy night, my first cries mixed with the moans of the wind. The winter storm was so fierce it knocked out Seattle's power. A rainy night in Seattle is not shocking news. It rains one out of four days here, so the Emerald City is often shrouded in a silver curtain of water. But it may shock some to know that the misty curtain hides a secret.

Seattle is haunted. But unlike some cities whose residents proudly trumpet their haunting, Seattleites are somewhat shy about sharing their spirit encounters. While residents of St. Augustine, Florida, New Orleans, Louisiana, and Savannah, Georgia, all claim that theirs is the "the most haunted city in America," Seattle could give them a run for their money.

One of the most haunted spots in Seattle is Pioneer Square. Settlers built here in the 1850s—right on top of the mudflats! Everything was fine when the tide was out, but when the frigid salty waters of Puget Sound crept in, things got messy, because the sewers flushed in reverse.

The hardy Seattle citizens lived with their plumbing problems until 1889 when a pot of glue fell over and sparked a fire. The flames swept through the town, destroying sixty-six blocks.

No people died, but an estimated one million rats were incinerated. The city was rebuilt and elevated, eliminating the plumbing problems.

Beneath the new city, the underground town remained and was eventually condemned, left to the rats and ghosts.

Then in the 1960s, writer William Spiedel spearheaded a project to save the underground realm, and today tourists can follow guides through the dark and musty streets below, see remnants of early buildings, and—if they are vigilant—glimpse specters from another time.

Tour guide Midge Markey was leading several dozen six-year-olds through the underground when she encountered something that sent a chill through her.

They had stopped below First Avenue and Yesler Way. Here in the shadowy world beneath, a heap of dusty bricks is a favorite frolicking sport for rats. Kids, she explains, always get excited about the rats, so she told them they should look carefully at the bricks. "You just might see a rat scuttling away," she remarked. While the children were busy looking for rats, she glanced at the old bank vault. There, beside it, stood a mustached man in old-fashioned attire. "His collar was buttoned up with tiny buttons, like the shirts in the 1800s," Midge told me.

Certain that the children would become hysterical at the sight of the ghost, she quickly turned her attention back to them, preparing to calm them down. But the kids were still searching for rats, oblivious to the ghost who had materialized beside them. Midge looked back at him, and he stared at her for a long moment before fading away.

"I thought I was losing my mind," she admits. "Then I saw him again, in the same spot a week later!"

While some of the other tour guides teased Midge when she confided

The huge arch in the Pioneer Building not only marks the beginning of the Underground Tour, but the spot where three men lost their lives many years ago. (Leslie Rule)

in them about her encounters, others have seen apparitions in the dank world beneath. Ghosts are also seen above ground.

Do they creep up from below?

Many of the area establishments have basements that connect to the underground, and the spirits of yesteryear are seen passing through. At Luigi's Grotto, a popular restaurant on Cherry Street, Luigi led me through his basement to an opening to the cavernous underground, then showed me a downstairs corner of the restaurant where a waitress once saw a woman materialize.

Is she the same woman who appears just a stone's throw away at the Broderick Building?

Women from the law offices whisper about the ghostly lady who visits the seventh floor. No one knows what the Victorian woman in voluminous skirts is looking for.

When I stopped in the Megan Mary Olander Flower Shop on First Avenue, I casually asked Megan if the shop had ghosts. She exchanged

Do those who suffered unjust deaths still roam the old streets? (Leslie Rule)

knowing glances with her employees before admitting, "We have a ghost who turns the radio on and off."

And in First Avenue's J&M Café, an employee was stunned to see a ghost in the basement. The specter stood beside the old ticket booth, which was left over from the days when the location was a trolley station. He looked as if he was planning to purchase fare. But he is out of luck. The last trolley left the station decades ago.

Who are the ghosts of Seattle's Pioneer Square?

Certainly they are left over from a variety of eras and met different fates, but if we are to embrace the theory that violent death results in the most ghosts, then a dark day in January 1882 is surely to blame.

When George Reynolds married lovely Mary Meydenbauer, everyone expected them to have a long and happy life together, but just weeks later, two killers snatched that away.

George was walking at Third Avenue and Marion Street when two men approached. James Sullivan and William Howard demanded his money. George reached for his revolver, but both robbers shot.

Young George crumpled to the sidewalk and died.

A row of windows in the Pioneer Building look down upon haunted Pioneer Square. (Leslie Rule)

Called to action by the clanging of the fire bell, two hundred determined men ran to search for the robbers. They combed the narrow streets, the shadowy woods, and the cold rocky beach in search of the killers. They drilled holes into the bottoms of all the small boats, so the murderers could not escape by water.

Four hours after the killing, the robbers were arrested, but the vigilantes wanted blood. They grabbed the guilty pair from the lawmen and carried them swiftly to the yard of prominent citizen Henry Yesler. There, a makeshift gallows had been made between two maple trees. With a frenzied crowd of two thousand shouting encouragement, Sullivan and Howard were lynched.

The execution made the crowd hungry for more, so the mob went to the jail for another prisoner, Benjamin Payne.

Benjamin was suspected of killing a policeman, but shortly before his death, the victim had insisted Payne was not to blame. On his deathbed, police officer David Sires had acknowledged he had failed to announce himself as he chased Payne through the dark Seattle streets. Payne, afraid a robber was after him, had shot Sires.

But the crowd was in no mood to listen to reason. Despite Sheriff Wykoff's protests, the mob broke down a jail wall and carried Payne to the gallows. "If you hang me, you'll hang an innocent man!" Payne cried, as angry hands slipped a noose around his neck.

Two days later, Sheriff Wykoff, burdened by the horror, died of a heart attack.

When the three lynched men were buried, the nooses were left around their necks, the long ropes sticking out above the dirt.

Some of Seattle's children sneaked to the grave sites and pulled at the ropes, snipping sections of it for souvenirs. In a macabre fashion statement, sweet-faced little girls braided pieces of the rope into their hair for school, and the boys tied pieces of the death rope to their suspenders.

The moon has set on Seattle over forty thousand times since that tragic day. All of the people involved are long dead.

Still, I wonder, what was it like to be there? What happened when the excitement died? Did everyone go home for supper? What did they see when they crawled into their beds and closed their eyes? Did the anguished faces of the dead men fill their dreams? Or did they sleep peacefully, smugly believing that justice was served?

Seattle's graceful pergola is a historic landmark, which sits atop the very haunted underground land. (Leslie Rule)

Mary Reynolds must have had nightmares. She had become a widow so soon after becoming a bride.

And what of her husband, the robbery victim? Did the young man who so suddenly lost his future go peacefully to the afterlife? Or is he still here, waiting in the underground, looking for Mary or his killers?

We have our choice of ghosts from that episode: Benjamin Payne, who mistakenly shot the policeman; David Sires, the policeman whom Payne shot; and robbers James Sullivan and William Howard. Any of them could still be lurking beneath.

Sheriff Wykoff, who succumbed to a heart attack, also could be down below, still trying to bring order.

The violence of their deaths makes them all candidates to live on as Seattle's underground ghosts. Perhaps one of them is the phantom who stared solemnly at tour guide Midge Markey.

What became of the women who loved the dead men? They, too, may be earthbound in the underground.

The site of the lynching has changed. Henry Yesler's house was demolished. The hanging trees are gone, too, perhaps made into furniture. Yes, it has changed, but the exact site is still known. In fact, it is the entrance to the Underground Tour.

Walk beneath the massive stone arch and down the wide gray stairs for a glimpse of a time long gone. And as you pass beneath the arch, remember that it marks the spot where horror happened on a January day over a century ago. Two thousand people chanted and cheered as three were hung. The executed trio passed through this spot on their way to the "other side." If you should meet them as you explore the underground realm, tell them their journey is not over. It is time for them to move along.

𝔊𝔥𝔬𝔰𝔱𝔰 𝔦𝔫 𝔱𝔥𝔢 𝔑𝔢𝔴𝔰

The Killer Wore Black

LISA POSLUNS, a thirty-eight-year-old real estate broker, met a terrible fate on November 3, 2002. She locked her fifth-floor office in the downtown Toronto building and prepared to go home to make her nightly phone call to her mother. A devoted daughter, she was also a devoted worker, who was known to slave over her desk for long hours.

Unfortunately, the wrong person had noted her schedule and was waiting for her when she stepped into the hallway.

He dragged the terrified woman to the basement, assaulted her, and then savagely stabbed her to death. The killer discarded her in the utility room, left his shoe print in her blood, and made his getaway.

Detectives were soon investigating the shocking murder and questioned everyone associated with Lisa and the building where she worked. Four months rolled by with no arrest in sight.

Apparently frustrated with the lack of progress, Lisa's ghost appeared to a janitor working in the building. According to the February 17, 2006, edition of the *Toronto Sun,* custodian Rui Marques testified that he was cleaning an office when she materialized and pointed to a black table. "I was trying to figure out what was the meaning of that," he told a Toronto court. "She pointed to the desk, and she faded away very quickly. The hair stood up on my arm."

A fellow custodian, Nelson DeJesus, usually wore black, so Rui Marques made a connection to the fact the spirit had pointed at a black table. It was a clue, he decided, and steered the police toward Nelson DeJesus.

Detectives followed up and gathered compelling evidence, including proof that the suspect's DNA matched that left at the crime scene.

Nelson DeJesus, thirty-six, was convicted of first-degree murder, with no chance of parole before 2028.

nine

Accidents Happen

What happens when another's carelessness causes a death? Is a dead person's spirit less insulted by the fact that their killer did not mean to hurt them?

Probably.

Still, fatal accidents seem to account for many earthbound spirits. Reports of hauntings around this sort of tragedy are countless. The popular theory among paranormal investigators is that the spirit is so shocked by a sudden death that it is unable to move on.

While natural disasters can be blamed on no one but a higher power, almost every other type of accident is the fault of someone. Often it is the victim himself. Other times it is a well-meaning person who made an unforgettable mistake.

I grew up beside one big, beautiful accident waiting to happen. Puget Sound was so near my home that on stormy days when the waves grew wild, the salty water splattered on our windows. When the sky churned, the waves turned a smoldering green as they rushed to crash upon the rocky beach.

On the days when Puget Sound shimmered blue, each white-ruffled wave glinted in the sunshine. Still, it was cold. At fifty-five degrees in the summer, the chill can cause a person to succumb to fatal hypothermia in five minutes.

I saw that as a challenge and was determined to swim to the light-house on Maury Island, two and half miles across the sound from my home. As a teenager, I thought of myself as a tough girl who could walk barefooted across barnacle-covered rocks without flinching. I'd done it so often that I had hardened the soles of my feet until they were thick and leathery.

Just as my feet could learn to take the sharp barnacles, my body could adapt to the cold. At age twenty, I acclimatized myself to the icy water by swimming in it daily, adding a few minutes each session until I could remain immersed for over two hours.

I planned my swim for the afternoon of a new moon, when the tide was the calmest. I coated myself with vegetable shortening to seal in body heat, and with two boats by my side, swam across the sound. Not a fast swimmer, it took me two hours and twenty minutes.

Though I was prepared, the average person is not.

While many people who live on Puget Sound wade into the waves on hot summer days, only the hardiest fully immerse themselves in the frigid water.

One poor soul took an unexpected dunk many decades ago and now lives on as a ghost of Puget Sound. I learned about him while my mother and I were signing books.

A woman came through the line and told us of an eerie encounter.

Years before, she and her husband had ventured out in a rowboat, and as they neared the shore of Maury Island, a storm hit, and the water grew wild. They were tossed about as they tried to avoid the big, jagged rocks. Cold water splashed into their boat, and they feared they would sink.

Suddenly, a fisherman appeared, wading toward them. "He grabbed the boat and pulled us in," the woman confided.

Once ashore, the man left so hurriedly that they did not see him go. Puzzled, the couple headed up a path to a small store. When they told the cashier about the mysterious man who had saved them, she was skeptical. "She told us that that part of the beach was deserted, and she had never known anyone like the old man we described."

They mulled over their experience. It had had a surreal quality to it. He had appeared and disappeared so quickly, it was as if he was a ghost. *A ghost.*

They were not prone to fanciful notions, yet they felt in their bones that they had met a ghost.

After the woman finished her account, I turned to my mother and said, "I wonder who he was. I don't remember a fisherman dying out there."

"Don't you remember?" my mother exclaimed. "It was one of your Grandma Doris's favorite stories!"

Doris Rule, my father's mother, had lived on the beach many years before. I didn't recall the story, but my mother did.

Sometime back in the 1940s, a fisherman had regularly fished in the waters between our beach and Maury Island. An obese woman began to pester him for a ride in his rowboat. He politely turned her down, but she kept asking until one day he gave in.

Unfortunately, the woman was so big that she tipped over the boat. The fisherman and his passenger were suddenly bobbing in the chill water. The woman's fat saved her life. It provided extra insulation and protected her from the cold.

But the fisherman quickly turned blue and was in the fatal grips of hypothermia before rescuers could reach him.

While I cannot be certain that the helpful mystery man who saved the couple was the spirit of the dead fisherman, it makes sense that he was. It was as if he were on a mission to save others from his icy fate.

Here are some more accounts of accident victims who remain earthbound.

Sunday Drive

Sometimes it is the smallest action that determines our fate. It can be something as simple as lingering over a second cup of coffee, forgetting to return a phone call, or passing another car on the road.

Normally not life or death decisions, we usually do not give these small acts a second thought. But when such a little thing prolongs our lives or brings swift death, we never forget them. It was Sunday, February 24, 1946 when Elmer Lawson of Charleston, South Carolina, made an unforgettable choice that irrevocably altered the lives of eight people and left a macabre apparition behind.

In 1929, Charleston became home to the fifth-longest bridge in the world with the building of a superstructure that spanned two wide waterways, Cooper River and Town Creek. At 2.71 miles long and 150 feet above the water, the bridge cut a beautifully intricate silhouette in the moonlight.

The John P. Grace Memorial Bridge, also known as the Cooper River Bridge, became a great convenience and a cherished landmark for area residents.

In February 1946, an enormous ship was anchored in Charleston Harbor, near the bridge. The *Nicaragua Victory* was a hulking ten thousand tons and not easy to maneuver.

One Sunday afternoon, the crew apparently misunderstood the captain's order to remove the slack from the anchor chains. Instead, they pulled the anchors up, allowing the monstrous freighter to drift.

Dorothy and Bill Clapper could not have known they were on a fatal path when they steered their green Chevrolet onto the Cooper River Bridge. The young couple had had a pleasant Sunday at the beach on the Isle of Palms and had enjoyed watching one-year-old Bill Jr. play in the sand. As the Clappers drove over the bridge, they did not notice the freighter plowing toward them. And, apparently, neither did the Lawson family.

Who knows what was in Elmer Lawson's mind as he decided to speed up on the Cooper River Bridge?

The thirty-seven-year-old father's green Oldsmobile was packed. Along for the trip were his wife, thirty-year-old Evelyn; his mother, sixty-year-old Rose; and his two small children. Robert was seven years old, and little Diana, only three.

As they reached the arch of the bridge, Elmer gave the pedal a little extra gas, and their car passed the Clapper family's vehicle. Dorothy glanced up to see the Lawson youngsters waving as they passed.

Why was Elmer in such a hurry?

We will never know. His simple decision to pass another car sentenced him and his family to a watery grave. Just after he overtook the Clappers, the runaway ship slammed into the bridge.

A 240-foot section of the bridge collapsed on impact, and the Lawson car shot off the road and plummeted to the river below.

The Clappers braked in the nick of time.

In a 2005 interview with Tony Bartlelme of Charleston's *Post and Courier*, Dorothy Clapper recalled the pivotal moment when the Lawsons passed them. "I told Bill that if that car hadn't passed us, we could have been the ones that drove off the bridge. . . ."

The newspaper also quoted Jesse Morillo, who was on board the ship. "I couldn't believe my eyes," he said. "When we hit the first section, it collapsed like a child's Erector Set. And we didn't slow down." As the car fell, he was horrified at the sight of two small children, their hands pressed against the windows.

The Lawson family was entombed in their car for days before their bodies were recovered.

Six months later, the bridge was repaired, and people tried to put the tragedy out of their minds as they traveled over it. While most succeeded, a few cannot forget, because as they traversed the Cooper

River Bridge, they found themselves side by side with a ghost car ridden in by the dead.

According to the guides of the Haunted Charleston Walking Tour, there has been more than one sighting of the ill-fated Oldsmobile.

One family of witnesses was headed home from an outing on a February day when they drove onto the bridge. They noticed an odd, out-of-date, green Oldsmobile ahead of them. The car kept starting and stopping, so the driver decided to pass the strange car. As they began to pass, they were startled by a shocking image.

Inside the vehicle was a lifeless family, dressed in 1940s fashion. In the front seat were a man and woman, with glazed and sunken eyes. The grandmother and two pale limp children sat in the back.

The terrified driver slammed on his brakes and allowed the ghostly car to pass him. It drove ahead and disappeared.

Is the Lawson family still trying to make it over the bridge?

Why does the car hesitate, stopping and starting so erratically? Is poor Elmer trying to relive that crucial moment that sent his family plummeting to their graves? Interestingly, he seemed to make the same decision he did on that black Sunday, when he passed the car of the startled family.

Let us hope that the souls of these poor folks have moved on, and that it is only a phenomenon called "a place memory" that witnesses see. The awful picture of five dead in a car may have been imprinted upon the environment, to appear when the conditions are optimal.

In this case, the witnesses were a family of five, traveling over the bridge in February, the anniversary month of the accident. This may have allowed the witnesses a morbid peek at a grisly snapshot in time.

After nearly eight decades of service, the old bridge was dismantled, replaced by an adjacent structure, the eight-lane Arthur Ravenel Jr. Bridge. Some ghost enthusiasts have speculated that this will not stop the death car from appearing. They theorize that there will soon be sightings of the Lawson family traveling through the air in the space the old bridge once occupied.

If you are easily frightened and you plan to drive over the Ravenel Bridge, maybe it is best to keep your eyes on the road.

"Help Me!"

No one knows the nooks and crannies of the Dundas District Public School better than the custodians. Built in 1929, the Hamilton, Ontario, school is spick-and-span—thanks to the hard-working staff and a ghost or two.

In the 1950s, five caretakers made a pact. Whoever was the first to die would return to haunt the others. Russell, the custodian who suggested the pact, was a perfectionist in charge of the third floor. He kept it spotless.

He eventually died and has apparently kept his word.

An employee who started work long after Russell's demise was assigned the third floor. One night, he got his bucket of soapy water ready and then decided to go to supper. He returned to find that the floor had been washed. "Russell did it!" his fellow employees insisted.

The same employee also saw the apparition of a tall man with a big smile. He appeared on the third floor, accompanied by the sound of jingling keys. It was most likely the ghost of Russell.

But what about the others?

Who are the five spirits seen on the back stairs? And who paces endlessly during the night? Most disturbing, who is the old woman?

Two custodians were preparing to leave one evening when they were chilled to the bone at the sound of an old woman's voice calling from the top of a staircase. "Help me," the voice cried.

It is one thing to have the spirit of a helpful cleaner in your midst; it is another when it is a mysterious old woman calling pitifully.

Perhaps she was a victim of the 1934 train wreck. The dead victims, locals say, were brought to the school, which was turned into a makeshift morgue.

The Christmas Day excursion train was filled with folks celebrating the joy of the season. Three hundred and ninety-seven passengers were returning to Toronto when the train was signaled to go onto a side rail so that another train could pass in Dundas.

The Maple Leaf, a Chicago to Montreal train, roared full speed into town. Its signal was green, an indication that the tracks were clear. Unfortunately, something went wrong with the switch, and the Maple Leaf torpedoed into the back of the excursion train. It telescoped into the last two wooden cars filled with people, killing most of them instantly.

At the horrendous sound of the crash, Dundas residents came running to help. They went into action, pulling the injured from the train, and ferrying them to the hospital. But work was slow because of the darkness.

The Christmas presents strewn about the track were a grim reminder of what the day was supposed to be. Rescuers tried not to think of the children who would never get to play with the toys that littered the ground.

The next day, newspaper headlines screamed that fifteen were dead. Thirteen were passengers and two were porters, all from the excursion train. Everyone aboard the Maple Leaf survived.

The accident was near the Dundas school, and its basement was quickly utilized as a morgue.

If time stands still for the dead, do those who wander the school think it is still Christmas Day 1934?

Spirits from the Sky

It was a black night in December 1972 when a jumbo jet took off from the John F. Kennedy International Airport in New York with 176 people on board. They thought they were destined for Miami, Florida, but instead they were destined for doom.

One hundred and one human beings would make a date with the Grim Reaper before midnight.

Captain Bob Loft and second officer Don Repo were family men and experienced pilots who did not take the safety of their passengers lightly.

The massive Lockheed L-1011 had served Eastern Air Lines for four months. Pilots and passengers marveled at the spacious luxury plane, with a tail that rose six stories high and a length that nearly spanned a football field.

The jet, however, had a few bugs that had yet to be explained to the pilots.

As Flight 401 approached Miami, the crew was blindsided by an unfortunate string of events. It began with a faulty warning light and culminated with mismatched readings of the altitude on the pilots' dual indicators. As the jet cruised on automatic pilot set to two thousand feet, one of the crew attempted to change a stuck light bulb. As he fiddled with it, the sensitive instrument panel was apparently jarred, and the autopilot became disengaged.

Despite the fact that the plane began to descend, the information was not accurately conveyed. As the jet dipped toward the earth, the utter darkness below offered no clue. The marshy Florida Everglades, swarming with gators and snakes, was cloaked in the shadow of night.

When Don Repo left the cockpit to check a potential problem with the landing gear, Captain Loft's indicator falsely assured him that the plane was high in the sky. He could not see the ground rushing toward them.

At 11:42 p.m. the plane crashed.

The story could have ended there, as do other aviation tragedies. Though horrible for those who lost loved ones, the fate of Flight 401 would have become a statistic if not for the determined spirits of the pilots who persevered beyond the grave and the writer who told their story.

The late John G. Fuller was a successful journalist and an admitted skeptic when he stumbled upon the amazing events that occurred in the wake of the tragedy.

Numerous employees of sound mind and body began to see the ghosts of the pilots killed in the crash. Pilots, flight attendants, and passengers all witnessed the apparitions of Bob Loft and Don Repo aboard Eastern Air Line's L-1011s.

In one instance, according to John Fuller, a stewardess approached a uniformed Eastern captain in the jump seat and said, "Excuse me, Captain. Are you jump-seating this ride? I don't have you on my list."

When the man did not respond, she politely persisted, but he stared straight ahead as if in a daze. With another attendant and passengers watching the drama unfold, she finally summoned the flight supervisor.

> *The flight captain leaned down to address the other captain, wrote the author. Then he froze. "My God, it's Bob Loft" he said. There was silence in the cabin. Then something happened that no one in the vicinity could explain. The captain in the first-class seat simply wasn't there. He was there one moment—and not the next.*

The most frequent sightings were of Don Repo. One attendant saw the distinct image of his face watching her from inside the luggage compartment. Several others reported that he had materialized near the microwave. Some said that his face stared at them from inside the microwave.

The materializations sometimes occurred as a warning when there were safety issues with the plane. At least one witness said Don Repo's ghost actually spoke to him, advising him of a problem. It was as if the pilots had remained to protect the passengers and flight crews from future dangers.

When they reported the encounters to Eastern Air Line's management, employees quickly realized it was the wrong thing to do. It was implied that those who so much as believed in ghosts were unbalanced, and their careers were threatened.

John Fuller's diligent research revealed that expensive parts of the ill-fated plane had been salvaged and recycled. The L-1011s, which received the recycled parts from the death jet, were the only ones where sightings were reported. Much of the activity centered on the microwave oven, which was recovered from the accident sight.

Eastern Air Line bigwigs must have realized the connection between the ghosts and the recycled parts, because they systematically and somewhat surreptitiously removed and replaced the haunted pieces.

When questioned by John Fuller and other members of the media, a spokesman for Eastern Air Lines denied that anything out of the ordinary had occurred on the planes. It was all made up, he contended.

Though John Fuller managed to interview numerous witnesses to the ghostly goings on, almost everyone spoke with him under the condition of anonymity.

As a writer of true ghost stories, this bothers me. I understand that the witnesses were afraid of ridicule and concerned for their jobs, but their unwillingness to stand behind their words detracts from the validity of the account.

I never met John Fuller and have no reason to doubt his words. He was a respected journalist, and he probably deserved his good reputation. But when an author uses so many pseudonyms, discerning readers can't help but feel niggling doubt.

Eastern Air Lines is no longer in business. Most of those who saw the ghosts of Flight 401 have likely switched careers or retired by now. If they would come forward and stand behind their testimonies, it would lend authenticity to Fuller's out-of-print, yet incredible book, *Ghost of Flight 401.*

I have made contact with just one person who knows anything about the haunted recycled plane parts. Leslie Cahier's son worked in a warehouse, which recycled salvaged plane parts. He mentioned to his mother that there was an abandoned microwave there. It sat beneath a tarp, no good use to anyone. Ask if you can take it home, she urged him. It was just the thing for her kitchen.

When he inquired, the response was quick and chilling. The microwave was not to be removed. It was the very one salvaged from the wreckage of Flight 401, the very one that had prompted the paranormal problems.

❧

Now, thirty years after the fascinating paranormal incidents related to Flight 401, spirits from the sky still walk among us. One of the latest reports of ghosts wrought from plane crashes comes from Africa.

Before they were ghosts, the victims were live human beings with the same needs and wants as the rest of us.

Nkiru Okoli, for instance, was twenty-two years old and expecting her first child. She and her husband, Chukwuemeka, had just finished their honeymoon in Ghana when she phoned her relatives. They had finally arrived back in Nigeria, she told them. They were on the last leg of the trip, about to board a Bellview airliner, Flight 201.

Nkiru asked her older sisters to meet them at the airport. And she had a special request for her mother: Could she make them yam porridge?

It was October 22, 2005, and Nkiru's family was excited about seeing her. Nkiru was a joyful person, and everyone was looking forward to watching her open her wedding presents, which waited, wrapped in pretty paper with shiny bows. She and Chukwuemeka were deeply in love, and there was so much to celebrate.

Meanwhile, another passenger, Remilekun Olaniyan, was preparing to board Bellview Flight 201, which her husband had begged her not to take, pleading that she instead wait until Monday. But she was in a hurry to reach her destination and stubbornly refused to change her plans.

And passenger Linus Sabulu, president of the National Association of Nurses and Midwives, had participated in the association's Nigerian conference and was so eager to return to his family, he made plans to take Flight 201, despite the fact his wife suggested he could stay over one more day and return home on Sunday.

The flight was full, and some travelers were frustrated when they were told that they could not board, that there was simply no room for them. They had no idea how lucky they were.

The 117 passengers who boarded Flight 201 on October 22 were mostly Nigerians, with one American and one Frenchman among them.

It was a stormy Saturday night as the Boeing 737 gathered power and rose into the sky, leaving the Labos airport behind. The twenty-four-year-old plane was bound for the Nigerian capital, Abuja. Soon after takeoff, the pilot issued a distress signal.

It was a hopeless cry for help.

Flight 201 crashed in the remote village of Lisa, killing all on board. The plane had been traveling at a tremendous speed and was buried on impact.

When TV crews arrived, they broadcast the horror for the world to see. The airplane that had been given a clean bill of health seven months before was now reduced to twisted chunks of metal. Luggage was ripped to bits. No one had had the faintest chance of survival.

Relatives of the victims went into shock. They could not believe their loved ones were dead. And, it may be, the victims themselves did not know that they were dead. Residents of Lisa began to see them.

The village of Lisa is thirty miles north of the ill-fated plane's take-off. The tragedy that put them in the news also wiped out their electrical power when cables were severed by the aircraft. But it was the haunting that was reported in the *Saturday Independent* on November 5, 2005.

Village council secretary Apostle Sikiru Lasisi told a reporter that he and a family member had witnessed the ghost of a victim walking past their home. "We live in fear when it gets dark," he said, "because the spirits of the victims in the plane crash keep roaming the whole village. . . ."

Another resident, Aremo Olubode, told the reporter that many women and children there were so frightened of the ghosts that they no longer slept in their own homes, opting instead to stay with relatives in neighboring villages.

Disembodied voices were heard at night, especially on the path that led to the crash site.

While most of the villagers respected the dead, a few heartless criminals had looted the plane, stealing valuables from the lifeless passengers before a recovery team could locate the crash site. Some wondered if the blatant disrespect could have riled the spirits.

The cries of the ghosts and the sight of wandering souls disturbed residents to the point that they lived in terror. "The situation has gone so bad that we no longer have the guts to walk at night, and if we do, it is usually in groups. If you doubt me, please spend a night with us here and experience what we go through every night," Aremo challenged the reporter.

As of this writing, the villagers have yet to have their power restored. There is no word on the status of the ghosts. Let us hope that they have come to terms with their deaths and have moved on to a peaceful place.

❧

Who knows how many tragic travelers are trapped in the nightmare of their doomed airplanes?

A horrible crash in Reno, Nevada, is yet another one for the books.

It was about one a.m., January 21, 1985, when Galaxy Flight 203 took off from what is today known as the Reno-Tahoe International Airport. The chartered flight held sixty-five passengers who were headed to Minnesota. Many of them had enjoyed a weekend of gambling in Lake Tahoe during the Super Bowl Sunday weekend. Tragically, the plane crashed in a field, shortly after takeoff.

Seventy passengers and crew members lost their lives.

The lone survivor was a seventeen-year-old Minnesota boy who was thrown free of the burning crash. He was found still strapped in his seat.

Today the area is covered by retail stores and parking lots. Let us hope that the spirits of the accident victims have been able to move on. That was not the case in the hours following the crash.

Paranormal investigator Debby Constantino spoke with a member of the recovery crew, who was on the site immediately after the crash. As he worked on the grisly task, ghosts of the dead wandered aimlessly through the wreckage. "He wasn't the only one who saw them," said Debby. "He said nearly everyone there witnessed apparitions."

Earthbound Accident Victims

Candid Camera

Employees of the Belfast print shop can't help but jump when they hear the frightened shrieks. But they know there is nothing they can do to help. The screams of the Irish teenager make the tiny hairs on their arms prickle. The poor girl has been dead for nearly a century.

In 1912 when Helena Blunden took her last breath, the sixteen-year-old could not have imagined the technology of the future. If she had lived a normal life span, one day she would have embraced inventions such as televisions and microwave ovens, and, perhaps, even cell phones and computers.

But when fate literally threw an obstacle in her path, these things were years from being introduced to the world. The day Helena died, no had ever heard of a "ghost cam."

What would Helena have thought if she had known that one day millions of eyes from around the earth would be trained on the place her life ended?

The ghostly goings on of Helena Blunden have become part of the focus of a hobby utilizing ghost cams. In countless haunted places throughout the world, video cameras have been set up and connected to the Internet so that ghost enthusiasts can watch twenty-four hours a day, seven days a week, if they choose.

People stare wide-eyed at their computers, trying not to blink lest they miss an apparition. Often, message boards are attached to the Web sites so that viewers can record their observations.

Helena Blunden had dreamed of being a star. Today, she is one of the stars of Ghost Watch, a Web site that features a ghost cam trained on the print shop where Helena's restless spirit roams. According to the folks who run the site, Helena toiled sixty hours a week in the place when it was a linen mill.

Her job was in the spinning room, and the cheerful girl hummed while she worked, despite the poor conditions. Summer days brought stifling heat, and it was not unusual for workers to faint there.

Helena, however, did not let the environment get her down. She had hopes for the future. She was going to be a singer. She loved music, and on Sunday, April 14, 1912, she had plans to go to a concert at the Grand Opera House immediately after work.

According to Ghost Watch, a grumpy old woman named Margaret was in charge of mopping the stairs. When a boy walked over the damp stairs, Margaret dropped her mop and proceeded to scold him.

Helena finished her work at seven p.m. and was headed down the stairs when she tripped over the forgotten mop. She toppled over the banister, screaming as she fell. The impact killed her instantly.

In addition to the sound of her disembodied screams, employees in the old building have reported the sound of Helena's humming. Sometimes her apparition materializes, and sometimes folks know she's around because items are mysteriously misplaced.

Since the live Web cam was installed in 1998, watchers regularly post their ghost sightings on the Web site. They record such paranormal happenings as boxes moving on their own, the press inexplicably running, and the appearances of ghosts.

www.irelandseye.com/ghost/index.shtm

Blue Bell Hell

In a scenario that sounds as if it came straight out of the plot of the 1960s hit television program *The Twilight Zone*, a driver in southeast England thought he had struck a young woman as he drove along a dark road in November 1992.

When the accident victim mysteriously vanished, the distraught driver went to the police, who returned with him to help search. When no victim could be found, it was concluded he had encountered a ghost.

Blue Bell Hill near Maidstone in Kent soon became notorious as a haunted spot when the figure materialized in the paths of at least two other vehicles that November.

Paranormal investigators speculate that the apparition belongs to a bride who was killed on the road on her way to her wedding in November 1965. Two of her bridesmaids also died in the car collision.

Newspaper articles chronicled the supernatural experiences, including the details of the encounter of one horrified driver who wrapped the victim in a blanket and placed her beside the road before rushing to get help. Upon return, the injured woman was missing.

The witness descriptions of the ghost varied. While some described the apparition as lovely and young, others shuddered as they remembered a shriveled screaming face.

It may be that all three of the women killed there are appearing, each taking on a different form. Or the bride may be materializing in varying moods. She had experienced a gamut of emotions on that fateful day, and witnesses may be sensing a range of these.

Paramount Joe

According to local lore, the Paramount Arts Center in Ashland, Kentucky, is haunted by a worker who died there in a freak accident.

In 1931 the historic building debuted as a plush movie theater, complete with a stage and heavy curtains. While workers were putting the finishing touches on the theater, a man died in a freak accident, say locals.

"Paramount Joe" was left alone in the building while the rest of the crew went to lunch. When they returned, they found he had been strangled in the ropes that operated the stage curtains.

While actual documentation of the death has eluded researchers, many have witnessed odd things there, and some have speculated that the dead man's spirit is still there. Does he blame the crew for abandoning him in his time of need?

Witnesses have seen the lights turn themselves on and off and heard the sound of heavy boots clomping across the empty stage. When Ghost Chasers International, a paranormal research team, investigated the old theater, its EMF meters picked up inexplicable energy, particularly on the stage.

PARAMOUNT ARTS CENTER
1300 Winchester Avenue

Ashland, KY

(606) 324-3175

www.paramountartscenter.com

Tragedy on Virginia Street

Owners of Cal Neva's Nevadan Hotel have plans to turn the building into a condominium complex. Reno ghost enthusiasts are waiting to see if the change will release the spirit of a woman stuck there for over three decades.

It was November 22, 1973, when a forty-seven-year-old Canadian woman had the misfortunate to be at the wrong place at the wrong time. She was strolling past the old Hilps Drug Store on Virginia Street as workers dismantled the building.

The building collapsed prematurely, dumping heavy debris onto passersby. Two people were injured, and the Canadian woman was killed.

When the hotel was later built on that spot, folks began to spy an attractive woman who was not of this world. The slender redhead wore bright red lipstick and smiled at those she encountered. A painter reported that while he was working in the basement men's room he heard the phantom steps of a high-heeled woman tapping across the tile floor.

Many believe that the friendly ghost belongs to the woman who died so suddenly when the building collapsed. If the new residents of the condominium should find the smiling ghost in their living room, a few kind words could help her to move along.

The Nevadan is on Virginia Street in downtown Reno, Nevada.

Ghosts in the News

Tea Dance Terror

ONE MOMENT THEY WERE DANCING, laughing, and sipping champagne; the next they were dead, dying, or searching desperately for loved ones. A shocking Kansas City, Missouri, accident in 1981 may have launched some spirits on a journey backward in time, according to an October 27, 2005, edition of the *Pitch*, a Kansas City weekly newspaper.

It was Friday night, July 18, 1981, and hundreds of people had gathered at the new Hyatt Regency for a "tea dance" in the lobby of the forty-story luxury hotel.

Some of the crowd moved to the skywalks, where they leaned on the railing and chatted with each other as they watched the dancing couples below. At 7:05 p.m. those on the fourth-floor skywalk had no time to react when the floor beneath them vanished. The fourth-floor skywalk pancaked onto the second-floor skywalk, directly below it, and that in turn crashed to the floor. While some people were instantly killed, others were trapped in the wreckage.

Firefighters and volunteers dug through the tangle of twisted steel, shattered glass, and debris, frantically trying to save those who cried for help. In the end 114 people were killed, and over 200 were hurt.

An engineer hired by the *Kansas City Star* soon discovered the flaw in the design that caused the catastrophe. While the original design was sound, with each skywalk suspended from the ceiling with six rods, a change was made so that the second-floor skywalk hung from the fourth-floor skywalk. The strain on the higher skywalk was simply too great, and it gave way.

In his 2005 article in the *Pitch*, writer Justin Kendall said that employees experienced a haunting at the hotel soon after the accident. He consulted two psychics who suggested that management may have secretly had the hotel cleansed of the energy left over from the trauma, as paranormal incidents reported there ceased shortly after the tragedy.

Justin Kendall also wrote that the late Kansas City ghost investigator Maurice Schwalm had difficulty snapping a photograph at the scene of the disaster. Each time he tried to take a picture, an unseen hand jerked the camera.

Oddest of all are the reports that Maurice Schwalm received prior to the tea dance tragedy. "Before the skywalks collapsed," wrote Justin Kendall, "Schwalm was getting calls from neighbors of the Hyatt claiming they'd had visions of couples dancing outside of their windows."

It is possible the spirits of those killed in the horrific accident were so disoriented that they stepped out of time to appear to those in the past.

ten

Overnight with Ghosts

Ghost enthusiasts are flocking to haunted hotels, inns, and B&Bs. In what other places can you have an entire night to encounter a specter and get room service? The longer you stay at a haunted place, the better your chances of having a paranormal experience. And if you get too scared, you can always check out!

The most haunted hotels tend to be those where murder was committed. Here are a few such places with dark histories where ghosts have been experienced.

No Vacancy

When I visited the Menger Hotel in the summer of 2005, I was there on assignment for *Reader's Digest* to cover the haunting by the murdered chambermaid.

The historic San Antonio hotel is filled with ghosts. People from across the country travel to Texas to check into the Menger in hopes of encountering one.

Since its grand opening in 1859, the Menger has had plenty of time to gather ghosts. Its proximity to one of the most famous bloodbaths in America probably adds to the spirit count. It sits adjacent to the Alamo, where men, women, and children suffered violent death in 1836.

The old hotel may cater to some of the troubled spirits who wander in. As for the other ghosts, their stories are as elusive as they are. And as hard as I tried to open my third eye for a glimpse of them, it stayed stubbornly shut.

Ernesto Malacara met a very unusual woman at the Menger Hotel. (Leslie Rule)

At first I was envious when I learned of the guest who met a century-old ghost at the hotel. But when I learned how she had developed her ability to peer into the other side, I knew it was not a price that I would pay.

The woman, according to hotel public relations director Ernesto Malacara, had a brain tumor that had heightened her psychic ability. Though the doctors told her that she was hallucinating when she confided that she could see ghosts, Ernesto believed her.

It was a stifling hot day when the guest strolled through the rotunda room, just off of the lobby. The marble floors there are so shiny they reflect like mirrors, and the view to the ceiling is dizzying. The balconies to the second and third floors circle the room, and towering pillars support them.

A woman in a heavy black dress appeared in front of the guest. The fashion was reminiscent of the late 1800s and not appropriate for a scorching summer day.

As the guest studied the out-of-place woman, she was surprised to hear her say, "I did not jump. I was *pushed*."

The ghost had indicated a corner of the balcony on the third floor, and Ernesto pointed it out to me.

Perhaps it was the power of suggestion, but I was not consciously thinking of it when I took photographs from the spot later. My mind was focused on framing an interesting shot.

Suddenly, I felt a strong sense of a presence and turned around, expecting to see another guest peering over my shoulder.

No one was there.

One night around midnight, I was wandering through the hotel, wishing for a paranormal encounter, when I glanced up at the third-floor balcony to see that the light in the questionable spot had burned out.

A moment later, it came back on. And then it winked off again. It repeated the pattern several more times over the next ten minutes while the other lights remained steadily burning.

Coincidence?

Maybe. But the fact that so many credible folks have come forward to share their encounters, makes me wonder if it was something more. A woman from long ago could have been shoved from the third-floor balcony. The railing is low enough that I got a case of vertigo whenever I got near it.

If there were no witnesses to the fatal push, the authorities may have believed it was a suicide. So far, my research has not turned up any old reports of a woman falling from the balcony.

One of the reasons that Ernesto Malacara believed the guest's account of the ghostly woman is that he, too, has met an interesting visitor there.

One day in the lobby, he noticed an elderly lady knitting. "She was sitting in a big chair," said Ernesto. "She wore a blue dress with hand-embroidered stars." He noted the uneven stars and thought the design was a little unusual. The dress looked homemade. She also wore a beret, with a dangling tassel. Her small, metal-framed glasses appeared to be antiques.

Ernesto approached the woman, explained that he was with the hotel, and politely asked, "Are you comfortable? Is there anything I can get you?"

Indignantly, the woman snapped, "I am just fine! Thank you!"

Suddenly, he found himself staring at the empty chair. She had vanished as quickly as a burst balloon.

"I wish I had noticed what she was knitting," he told me, explaining that that one detail could have been the clue to the mystery of her identity. Sometime later, a psychic visiting the hotel gave him a description of the same ghost.

The Crockett Hotel, on the street behind the Menger, is not immune to paranormal activity. I spoke with an employee there who told me of a family that had made a special point to return for a second visit.

View from the second floor of the Menger's Rotunda Room. A ghost shared a shocking secret with a guest about the third-floor balcony. (Leslie Rule)

The Menger Hotel may be one of the world's most haunted hotels. (Leslie Rule)

The Alamo's tragic history populated the entire area with ghosts. (Leslie Rule)

Perhaps some ghosts don't want to "remember the Alamo" and choose instead to reside at the elegant Menger next door. (Leslie Rule)

How many of the ghosts seen at the Menger Hotel were killed at the nearby Alamo? (Leslie Rule)

"Our daughter wanted to play with her friend again," the guests had informed the employee. The little girl was about five years old and had had such a great time with her friend that she had talked about her non-stop and begged her parents to take her back to the Crockett Hotel.

The parents had never seen their daughter's friend. But they saw their child's eyes light up as she giggled in delight at the antics of an unseen presence.

The friend was a ghost.

The spirit of the little girl was a forever five-year-old and must have been tickled to have a playmate who could see her. Her identity remains an enigma, though I suspect that she was one of the children slain in their beds during the Alamo attack.

THE MENGER HOTEL

204 Alamo Plaza

San Antonio, TX 78205

(210) 223-4361

www.mengerhotel.com

Secrets in the Attic

On a quiet summer day in 2002, ghost hunter Janice Oberding visited one of her favorite haunted places. She had brought her son, Brad, and daughter-in-law, Peggy, along for the adventure.

As they drove up the hill to St. Mary's Art Center in Virginia City, Nevada, they noticed that the big old house looked deserted.

"I don't think there is anyone here today," said Janice.

Her son pointed to the center attic window. "No, there is someone here," Brad protested. "I just saw someone standing at the window."

Janice glanced at the window but did not see anyone there.

Perhaps whoever Brad had seen was now running down the stairs to let them in. They rapped on the door and waited for a long moment on the big porch.

Finally, the caretaker came around the side of the house. He had been in a back room, he said. Asked about the figure in the attic, he shook his head. He was the only one there, and he had not been in the attic all day.

Janice knew it was not the first time that ghostly eyes had watched visitors from the attic. "Many people have reported seeing a nun standing at that window," she told me.

Folks who know St. Mary's Art Center are not surprised to hear reports of apparitions there. The place is extremely haunted. and is popular with ghost hunters. The entire house can be rented out for a weekend and is a favorite place for ghost investigators' paranormal slumber parties.

Built as a hospital in 1876 by the Sisters of Charity, the site had previously been Van Bokklen's Beer Gardens. The mountainous land once echoed with drunken laughter as the beer flowed.

Owner Jacob Van Bokklen was killed in an explosion in 1873. Some folks wonder if his ghost is among those who wander the rooms of St. Mary's Art Center.

A variety of art classes are taught at the nonprofit center, and the creative people who frequent the place may be more open to the idea of ghosts than most.

"The ghost of the nun is seen most often," said Janice, who explained that visitors to the center find the specter in white to be kind and gentle. "They usually see her in room 11. One student entered her room and was startled to see the nun sitting on her bed."

As the stunned student stared, a sad smile touched the nun's lips, and then she vanished.

But it was not the last she would see of her. That night, when the student was in bed, the nun again appeared and gently pulled the blankets up around the woman's chin.

Who peers from this window of St. Mary's Art Center when all living people have vacated the premises? (Leslie Rule)

A heavy snow falls upon the St. Mary's Art Center, where the ghost of a nun wanders. (Leslie Rule)

Overnight guests at St. Mary's Art Center are sometimes startled to find a ghost tucking them in. (Leslie Rule)

Debby Constantino, an electronic voice phenomena expert, is in the attic of St. Mary's Art Center preparing to communicate with spirits. She and her husband, Mark, have captured ghostly voices on tape in the old haunted house. (Leslie Rule)

Some say the apparitions seen on the premises of St. Mary's Art Center were victims of a long-ago fire. (Leslie Rule)

St. Mary's Art Center's huge porch welcomes both the living and the dead. (Leslie Rule)

Others have encountered the ghost of a hefty woman in the kitchen. She materializes with the distinct scent of violets surrounding her.

What happened at the house to cause so much activity?

Maybe the spirits are left over from the days the building was a hospital. Overnight visitors have been startled awake by someone trying to take their temperatures. And they have heard the squeaking wheels of a gurney as it rolls past their rooms in the dead of night.

But something else likely causes the ghostly activity, Janice said. "There was a terrible fire there," she explained. "Many people were killed, including a nun."

The nun was a hero. She helped many people out of the burning house and continued to go back in to rescue more.

The last time she rushed back into the house she did not come out.

St. Mary's Art Center has a welcoming feel about it. It is unpretentious and cozy, with a hodgepodge of funky furniture that fills the main floors.

The attic, however, is another story.

When paranormal investigator Debby Constantino and I ventured into the attic, we felt uncomfortable. In one cramped storage area, we each had the sense that something bad had been done to a child there.

Most visitors to St. Mary's Art Center report that the guest rooms have a wonderful aura, and that the spirits there do not frighten them. (Leslie Rule)

Sensitive people often feel uneasy in the attic of the art center. (Leslie Rule)

We later learned that others have sensed the same thing in that spot.

And in one of the larger attic rooms, we both felt so anxious that we could barely breathe. When we told Janice about our reaction, she said, "That's where the mental patients were. They kept them chained in the attic."

At least one patient had been chained during the fire, she said. He perished there when he could not break free.

St. Mary's Art Center is in Virginia City, just off "R" Street
PO Box 396
Virginia City, NV 89440
(775) 847-7774

Lizzie

"Hi. This is Lizzie. No one can take your call now. Father's taking a nap on the sofa, and Abby is visiting a friend . . ." The bed and breakfast's macabre telephone announcement makes the flesh crawl.

"Father is taking a nap on the sofa . . ."

It is exactly what Andrew Borden was doing when he was bludgeoned with an axe on August 4, 1892, in his home in Fall River, Massachusetts. His wife, Abby, was killed in her room upstairs, and Lizzie was blamed for the grisly murder of her father and stepmother. Though a jury later acquitted her, she remained guilty in the public eye.

Today, the site of America's most infamous double murder is the Lizzie Borden Bed & Breakfast. The house has been carefully restored to resemble the time of the killing. It has been decorated with historical accuracy. Crime scene photographs were referenced so that furniture could be placed exactly as it was the day of the homicide.

It's no wonder the ghosts are confused! If the ghost of Andrew

Borden were to ask himself if perhaps he was dead, he'd likely look around and say, "Don't be silly. There's my sofa! Time for another nap!"

Indeed, an employee witnessed a fog form in the kitchen. The stunned woman watched as the wispy white entity floated into the parlor toward the sofa.

"She was a little unglued," said Lee Ann Wilber, owner of the Borden home since June 2004, adding that the previous owner had seen the specter of a woman in Victorian dress in the cellar.

Though Lee Ann has not yet seen a ghost there, she has experienced odd things. "I was in the basement when something touched me," she confessed. It was as if invisible fingers tapped her between her shoulder blades and then moved down her back.

Does Lizzie haunt her childhood home?

No.

At least that is what Lee Ann believes. "Lizzie is not here," she said adamantly. It is the murder victims who remain frozen in time in the historical home.

The killing was so long ago it is hard to wrap our minds around the fact that Andrew and Abby Borden were real people.

Yet they were.

Andrew Borden and his first wife, Sarah Morse Borden, had three daughters: Emma, Alice, and Lizzie. Little Alice died before Lizzie was born. When Lizzie was just two years old, her mother died.

Andrew later married Abby Durfee Gray. Gossips whispered that he could not love the chubby woman; that he had married her simply to get a free housekeeper and babysitter. Lizzie and Emma never liked their stepmother.

Many have said that when Andrew, a wealthy banker, put a piece of property in Abby's name, his daughters' anger toward their stepmother intensified. Andrew, they say, was so miserly that his daughters were frustrated by his refusal to supply them with the finer things, including indoor plumbing.

As members of one of the prominent families in town, Lizzie and Emma longed to live up on the hill among the wealthy Fall River residents.

Was it this frustration that fueled Lizzie's habit of stealing?

In addition to shoplifting in stores, she was the main suspect when valuable items, including diamonds, disappeared from her parents' room.

There is no one left alive to truly understand the intricacies of the Borden family dynamics, yet many are still speculating on them and the impact they had on the warm summer morning that stained the calendar with a splotch of blood that a century of sunny days cannot wipe clean.

The Borden housekeeper, Bridget Sullivan, was in her attic room on the fatal morning she heard Lizzie yell, "Come downstairs! Father is dead! Somebody got in and murdered him!"

Andrew Borden was on the sofa, covered in blood. Abby, too, was soon found dead in her upstairs room, apparently cut down as she made the bed. Andrew had received ten blows, while Abby suffered nineteen.

Emma Borden had an alibi. She was out of town. Fingers were soon pointing at thirty-one-year-old spinster Lizzie. Her case was not helped when a pharmacist testified that Lizzie had tried to buy prussic acid, a deadly poison, one day before the killing.

And Lizzie certainly looked guilty when her neighbor, Alice Russell, said she had seen Lizzie burning a blood-stained dress days after the homicide. The defense insisted the stains were not blood. They were paint.

Emma and other witnesses took the stand to say the stains on the cheap dress were indeed paint, left by careless painters who had worked in their home months before the murder.

As for rumors of contention in their family, said Emma, they were just that: rumors. The family was civil to each other, she testified. She suggested that a supposed rift between her and Lizzie that had been noted in the newspapers had been planted there by the police.

The defense also brought up the mysterious stranger who witnesses had seen lurking near the Borden home around the time of the killing. Maybe he was the killer!

Had the brutal murder been committed by a total stranger thirsty for blood? Had he taken the murder weapon with him when he slipped away?

Despite an exhaustive search, investigators could not be certain they had found the murder weapon. A hatchet with a broken handle was discovered in the cellar, and though primitive forensics indicated a match, it was not a certainty.

Searchers took apart walls within the Borden house, but to this day, the question of the murder weapon is part of the puzzle.

During the 1893 trial, the victims' skulls were revealed. Lizzie took one look at the gruesome sight and fainted. Was she really distressed, or was it a calculated move? If it was simple theatrics, it worked. The all-male jury deliberated for sixty-eight minutes and pronounced her not guilty. Somehow, they could not find the soft-spoken Sunday school teacher capable of such a grisly crime. On June 20, 1893, Lizzie was free to go.

Abby and Andrew, however, are not free. They are frozen in time, shadow people, hidden in the whispers of those who sit up all night at the B&B, debating America's most famous whodunit.

Shadow people are welcome at the popular B&B. In fact, many guests seek the place out because of the ghostly encounters.

Despite warnings that it could open the door to evil, a Ouija board is available for guests who dare to contact the other side. Regular séances also are conducted.

"We recently had a birthday party for a fourteen-year-old," Lee Ann told me, explaining that they held a séance as part of the entertainment. "It was in the dining room where the temperature is always comfortable." Yet, during the séance, an inexplicable cold breeze blew from nowhere, swirling around the teens until they shivered. The entire downstairs was soon chilled.

Another recent occurrence left Lee Ann shaking her head. She was in Abby's old room, making the bed for a couple who had spent the night and were out exploring. She tidied the room and was preparing to leave when she saw a pair of diamond earrings sparkling at her feet. "They were side by side on the floor by the door, as if someone had put them there," Lee Ann told me.

Why hadn't she noticed them when she entered the room?

She put the valuable earrings in her pocket for safekeeping. When the guests returned that evening, Lee Ann approached the wife as she relaxed in the parlor and asked, "Are you missing something?"

The woman perched on the sofa asked, "What do you mean?"

Lee Ann held out the earrings. "Her mouth popped open in surprise and her hands went to her ears," said Lee Ann. "Her husband had given them to her years ago, and she had never taken them off."

Later, the same woman was in the shower when she felt her necklace loosen and drop to her feet. She scooped it up as the suds swirled around it. It, too, had not been off her neck in years.

Whose ghostly hand tried to snatch the glittering jewelry?

Lizzie's!

Despite Lee Ann's belief that Lizzie is not one of the resident ghosts, the fact that Lizzie had a reputation for stealing diamonds makes me wonder.

Would Lizzie be more welcome if she were not an axe murderer?

After her acquittal, Lizzie was ostracized in Fall River. She purchased a big house on the hill, and though her neighbors found it pretentious, she named it Maplecroft. She further annoyed Fall River citizens when she changed her name to Lizbeth and entertained famous actors and actresses at home.

She broke the rules of a Victorian society, but that does not make her a killer.

A nurse who cared for Lizzie years after the tragedy said that her patient had confessed the truth to her. She had had a boyfriend that Andrew did not approve of. It was he who had committed the brutal double homicide.

If this is true, what happened to him? Did she continue to see him after the trial, sneaking off to a faraway city for rendezvous? Or did she break it off, sickened by what he had done but afraid to report him for fear she would be implicated in the plot?

In America, we are "innocent till proven guilty." Yet, Lizzie, never proven guilty, is rarely considered innocent. If she were innocent, would that draw her back to the scene of the crime? Is she roaming restlessly there, as visitors sit up all night debating her guilt?

Innocent or guilty, her ghost may very well be drawn to her childhood home. And she may not be alone. Could one ghost be responsible for so much paranormal activity?

Shadowy figures dart through the house, furniture moves on its own, and unseen hands tamper with the thermostat. Some have reported the sound of marbles rolling on the upper floors.

Marbles?

Yes, Lizzie may have lost hers, but these marbles are believed to belong to the ghosts of two neighbor children drowned by their mother. Some say the lonely little spirits seek refuge in the Borden house.

I've yet to find any documentation of the case, but Lee Ann insists there is a childish energy present in her B&B. The mischievous kids play with the thermostat, she said, turning it up or down on a whim.

The children's ghosts, she said, may have moved from the house that they shared with their murderous mother.

Lizzie Borden Bed & Breakfast

92 Second Street

Fall River, MA 02721

(508) 675-7333

www.lizzie-borden.com

Night on the Town

It was a quiet night at the Radisson Hotel in Boston, Massachusetts. As the security guard performed his routine check of the sixth floor, he paused and looked around.

Everything was as it should be. The floor reserved for conferences was still. The doors were all locked. The smiling people with their notebooks and name badges had all gone back to their rooms on other floors. He glanced at the wall, where his own shadow had paused with him.

Suddenly, a chill swept through him. *The shadow was walking away without him.* He spun around to see who had crept up behind him. There was no one there.

Who had cast the mysterious shadow?

November 28, 1942, was a cold night. But that did not stop Bostonians from stepping out on the town. Crowds gravitated toward a popular nightclub in the city's theater district.

The Cocoanut Grove on Piedmont Street was the closest thing to a tropical oasis in the middle of a Massachusetts winter. Fake coconut trees "grew" between the tables where customers crowded to sip cocktails. The ceiling was painted to look like a starry sky.

With the rattan-covered walls and island-themed drinks, a bit of liquor-fueled imagination could almost make people feel that they were in an exotic place.

That evening it felt balmy. Maybe it was the body heat. Customers were jammed close together, good-naturedly jockeying for tables.

To some, it was stifling. Many latecomers took one step inside and decided it was too hot and too crowded to stay. They went back into the icy air to find another place to celebrate Saturday night.

Those who stayed looked forward to hours of entertainment. Comedians, singers, and dancers all performed at the Cocoanut Grove.

Entertainers that evening included Buck Jones and Dotty Myles.

Cowboy Buck Jones, fifty-three, was a movie star and a veteran of World War I. In town on a war bond–selling tour to aid soldiers in World War II, he was busy doing good deeds. Just hours earlier, he had visited a children's hospital to cheer up his young fans.

Dotty Myles was a seventeen-year-old singer. She hoped that her gig at the Cocoanut Grove was the start of an exciting career. Lovely and talented, everyone said she would become a big star.

The club boasted three bars. The Caricature Bar and the Broadway Lounge were on the main floor, while the Melody Lounge and the kitchen were tucked into the basement.

At a little after ten p.m., bartender John Bradley called to sixteen-year-old bar boy Stanley Tomaszewski and pointed to one of the palm trees in the Melody Lounge. The lights were out beneath the palm fronds there. The customers seated at the table beneath it had apparently unscrewed the bulbs so that they could sit in the shadows.

Following the bartender's orders, the teenager went to fix the light. As he stood on a chair and peered up at the lightbulb, the couple at the table laughed and asked him to leave it dim. That decision, however, was not up to him.

Stanley could not see well enough in the dark to tighten the bulb. In the next instant, he did something that many believe dramatically and irrevocably altered the lives of too many people to count.

He lit a match.

It took a moment for the world to turn inside out. Stanley tightened the bulb and left the customers in a pool of cold light. Then he walked away.

When Stanley looked back and noticed the sparks on the fronds of the tree, they really didn't look very dangerous. He figured he could easily extinguish the sparks.

When the tree went up in flames, some of the people laughed as the boy tried to beat out the fire with his hands. Someone threw water on the fire, but the ceiling was soon ablaze. Before people could respond, a ball of fire rolled through the Cocoanut Grove nightclub.

Moments earlier Dotty had been studying her algebra book as she waited for her turn to sing. When the fire raged, the girl tried to flee, but she was knocked down by a herd of screaming people.

Meanwhile, some folks who knew they should leave the burning building figured there was time to get their hats and coats and headed for the cloakroom instead of the exit doors.

It was a deadly detour.

Some people ran toward the kitchen, searching for a way out. A few huddled in the walk-in freezer. Others managed to squeeze out of the tiny kitchen windows.

Katherine Swett refused to leave her cashier's box and stayed put to guard the money. She was later found dead.

As luck would have it, firefighters were nearby extinguishing a car fire and arrived on the scene quickly. They went to work, trying not to think of the charred victims piled up outside the nightclub.

When rescuers entered the building, they were startled by the sight of customers sitting calmly at their tables, their hands still curled around their drinks.

What were they waiting for? Why hadn't they fled the club as the others had?

But as their eyes adjusted, the firefighters realized that the people were lifeless. Poisonous gases had killed them so swiftly they had had no time to react. They did not know what had hit them.

Theirs were merciful deaths compared to some of the others. Witnesses described beautifully dressed women, shrieking as their evening gowns went up in flames. While many were burned to death, others were trampled by the stampede of panicked people. Some choked on the black smoke.

The Cocoanut Grove was a death trap. Terrified victims funneled toward the doorway, but the revolving doors allowed few to escape.

That exit soon became jammed with bodies. The last man out looked back to see the person behind him go up in flames.

The other exits were locked from the outside. Stacks of human beings were found just inside these doors, a sight that made firefighters cry.

Rescuers pulled countless people from the building. While some were shuttled to the hospital, the deceased were tossed into piles. In the confusion, a few live folks were thrown into the carnage, only to awaken later to a nightmare.

Within twelve minutes of the time the sparks were noticed, more than 490 people were dead or dying.

It was the worst death toll a fire had ever visited upon Boston.

Dotty Myles was found crumpled on the floor and carried to safety by a fireman. Her burns required years of medical treatment, including seventeen operations to restore her face. But she inspired many when she continued with her singing career and eventually went back to performing in clubs.

Cowboy Buck Jones made it out of the club but was burned so badly that he later died in the hospital, his name added to the growing list of the mortally wounded.

With the public crying for justice, the stern finger of the law was soon leveled at the greedy club owners who had put profit before safety. Each of the accused seemed to have an excuse or someone else to blame.

One boy told the truth. With the weight of the grief and anger of an entire city on his young shoulders, Stanley Tomasqewski told authorities that his match may have sparked the fire.

He was put into protective custody. Outraged relatives of the dead wanted revenge, and it was feared the teenager could be the next victim of the Cocoanut Grove tragedy.

The cause of the fire has been a great source of debate. Some believed that it was not the match, but a problem with the wiring installed by an unlicensed electrician. Others think that methyl chloride gas, used in the club's refrigerator, was a factor in the inferno.

Whatever the cause, Stanley carried the burden of the tragedy with him until the day he died at age sixty-eight in October 1994. Though Stanley was never held legally responsible for the fire, at least one bitter person would not let him forget. The cruel anonymous phone calls never ceased.

Club owner Barnett Welansky did not escape unscathed. He was found guilty of involuntary manslaughter and was sentenced to twelve to fifteen years in prison. He later suffered from cancer and was released early to die in peace.

Barnett's prosecution was an empty victory for the relatives of the victims. And the new safety laws and medical discoveries in the wake of the fire were not much comfort. They will never know how many lives their hapless family members saved.

Thanks to the 1942 tragedy, exits in public places are today clearly marked and unlock from the inside. Doctors used innovative procedures on the Cocoanut Grove burn victims that greatly advanced the knowledge for future care of such patients.

The information gleaned from the Cocoanut Grove fire has had a positive effect on future generations. Are those who died in the long-ago fire aware of that?

Perhaps many of them are aware. Perhaps they are in a peaceful place and happy that they could help others.

But a few stragglers remain.

Shocked and confused, still trying to find their way to safety, the ghost victims of the fire roam the site of the tragedy. Despite the fact that a luxury hotel, complete with its own theater, has been built on the deadly spot, energy from the horror may remain.

Wendi Clarke, human resources manager at the Radisson Hotel Boston, is well aware of the hotel's haunted reputation. While she has yet to encounter a ghost there, she has heard from those who have.

"An employee saw the ghost of a woman on the sixth floor," she told me.

The man had been cleaning up after a conference when he saw the apparition. He assumed she was a guest but could not understand where she had come from.

The conference floor was locked, and only the cleaning crew was there.

"He was really confused," remembered Wendi.

The woman disappeared as swiftly as she had appeared, leaving the cleaner with a story he could tell his grandchildren.

A plaque on the Radisson's Stuart Street Playhouse marks the spot of Boston's most fatal fire. (Leslie Rule)

Wendi steered me toward the hotel's theater, the Stuart Street Playhouse, which sits in an adjacent building. "Employees have seen the ghost of a man there," she told me.

Those working in the ticket booths the day I visited confirmed that the theater was haunted. Much of the paranormal activity there centered on water, they pointed out.

There have been inexplicable floods in the building, they said. And they once found a sopping wet seat. The theater had been vacant, and no one could figure out where the water had come from.

A water faucet on the second floor of the theater is notorious for turning itself on.

It is as if a panicked fire victim is still trying to extinguish the flames.

Others told me that those working alone in the theater at night have often heard disembodied voices calling their names.

Jacques, a longtime bar that today features performances by men in drag, served as a makeshift morgue on the night of the deadly Cocoanut Grove fire. A stone's toss from the back doors of the theater, the bar has long had a reputation for being plagued by the ghosts of the victims of the 1942 blaze. Though the employees openly admitted that the bar was haunted, they were tightlipped when it came to sharing their own ghostly encounters.

Most of the fire's victims have probably moved on, but the paranormal events indicate that at least a few ghosts remain.

In the Radisson's restaurant, the Theatre Café, bartender Edward Gormely has sensed their presence. Odd noises, he told me, emanate from the kitchen.

One night as he was carrying dirty dishes into the kitchen, he was startled by a sudden pop, accompanied by a flash of light. "It was right in front of my face," he said.

He turned to the chef and asked, "Are you messing with me?"

But the chef also looked startled. "I don't know what that was!" he exclaimed.

The noise had sounded like a balloon popping, and the light was as bright as fire.

The ghostly woman who walks the halls of the Radisson could be any one of the women who died in the Cocoanut Grove. I wonder if she is the spirit of Katherine Swett, the cashier who steadfastly stood by the club's money, even as the walls around her went up in flames.

Jacques's horrific night as a makeshift morgue left a legacy of tragedy and ghosts that few like to talk about. (Leslie Rule)

Those who knew her said that she feared her boss, Barnett Welansky, who worried over every nickel. His temper apparently frightened her more than fire.

Is she still looking for the cash box? Does she still fear that Barnett will be angry if she loses track of the money?

RADISSON HOTEL BOSTON & STUART STREET PLAYHOUSE
200 Stuart Street

Boston, MA 02116

(617) 482-1800

www.radisson.com/bostonma

Evil Riches

When the Goldfield Hotel opened its doors in 1908, it was considered the grandest hotel in the state of Nevada. The pride of the town of Goldfield with its marble floors, gilded columns, and shimmering crystal chandeliers, it catered to those who struck it rich in the mines.

The hotel was built atop a depleted gold mine. According to legend, it became the site of a horrible deed in the 1930s when Elizabeth, who worked as a prostitute, became pregnant.

The wealthy owner of the hotel was the father, but he wanted no part of it. He chained poor Elizabeth to the bedpost in room 109, holding her prisoner until the infant was born.

Some say that he then murdered Elizabeth and tossed the child down a mine shaft. It was a heartbreaking tragedy—one her soul has not yet grasped, for witnesses claim they have seen her apparition still chained to the bedpost and stalking the halls of the old building.

She floats along in a white nightgown, searching for her baby, whose pitiful cries can also be heard.

Psychics have detected numerous ghosts in the hotel and have pro-

A vintage postcard captures the image of the haunted Goldfield Hotel. (author's collection)

nounced the location as a portal to the other side, a kind of cosmic doorway where ghosts pass through.

THE GOLDFIELD HOTEL

On the corner of Columbia Street and Crook Avenue
Goldfield, NV

As of this writing, new owners of the Goldfield Hotel are making plans to renovate and reopen the historic building.

Knapp Time

The Mason House Inn, built in 1846 in Bentonsport, Iowa, is home to a number of ghosts, including that of Mr. Knapp, a guest from long ago who has never checked out.

He had a bit too much to drink one night and stumbled into the wrong room. According to an old newspaper account, poor Mr. Knapp did not realize his mistake until something plunged into his chest.

The guest he had disturbed assumed he was being robbed and pulled a saber from his walking stick and stabbed the hapless intruder.

The owners of the formidable brick inn believe that Mr. Knapp is still looking for his bed. They often hear shuffling footsteps upstairs, and when they investigate the empty upper floors, they find freshly made beds have been mysteriously messed up.

MASON HOUSE INN

21982 Hawk Drive

Bentonsport, Keosauqua, IA 52565

(319) 592-3133

www.masonhouseinn.com

Heartbreak Hotel

The historic Hotel San Carlos in downtown Phoenix, Arizona, is a favorite destination for ghost hunters, some of whom have encountered the specter of a heartbroken ghost who ended her life decades ago. Built in 1928, the hotel has the grand distinction of playing host to luminaries such as Clark Gable, Spencer Tracy, Carole Lombard, and Mae West, who all stayed at the hotel.

But the star of the Hotel San Carlos was not famous in life. She was simply sad—so sad that she decided to end it all. Her ghost is a big draw for the guests who travel from all over in hopes of an encounter with her.

According to area ghost enthusiasts, twenty-two-year-old Leone Jenson was so hurt when her love rejected her that she leapt from the seven-story hotel roof. She was clad in a lovely evening gown, perhaps anticipating a night on the town with her love, a bellboy who worked at another hotel. He, however, had found a new girlfriend. Crushed, the suicidal woman went to the roof and leapt.

Leone's misty figure has been seen by many throughout the years. And when guests and employees experience sudden blasts of cold air from nowhere, they believe it is Leone, making her presence felt.

***

HOTEL SAN CARLOS

202 North Central Avenue

Phoenix, AZ 85004

(866) 253-4121

www.hotelsancarlos.com

Haunted Ghost Town

Garnet, Montana, is a ghost town in the literal sense. The once-bustling mining community in the Garnet Mountain Range, east of Missoula, had a population of one thousand people in 1898. Those striking it rich with gold could spend their wealth at four stores or stay at one of the town's four hotels.

Though the pioneers are long dead, they are still seen and heard in Montana's most intact ghost town. Visitors have reported encountering folks in old-time clothes on Garnet's dirt roads. But as they draw close, the figures vanish.

Disembodied voices and music reportedly emanate from the remaining hotel.

Who are the ghosts of Garnet?

One may be the cofounder of the Nancy Hanks Gold Mine, the natural resource that launched the town. After selling his share to his partner, the man committed suicide.

Or he could be poor George Black, who was killed when he was thrown from his horse as he was riding through town.

Perhaps the disgruntled spirit of Michael Finn is still hanging around. After his death in Garnet in 1870, his drunken pals were carrying

Visitors to Garnet, Montana, are sometimes startled when they encounter ghosts here. (Leslie Rule)

his body for burial when they lost him in the river. When they went back to search for him the next day, they found him upside down in the water.

Two rustic cabins are available for overnight stays a few months out of the year. Run by the Garnet Preservation Association and the Bureau of Land Management of Montana, the rates are very reasonable, but conditions are primitive.

Overnight guests must enjoy nature and be ready to meet a ghost!

BUREAU OF LAND MANAGEMENT
Cabin Rental Program
3255 Fort Missoula Road
Missoula, MT 59804
(406) 329-3914
www.garnetghosttown.org

The road to Garnet, Montana, is sometimes traveled by ghosts. (Leslie Rule)

Are ghosts still living it up at the old dance hall in Gamet? (Leslie Rule)